Why We Better Lead and Lead Better

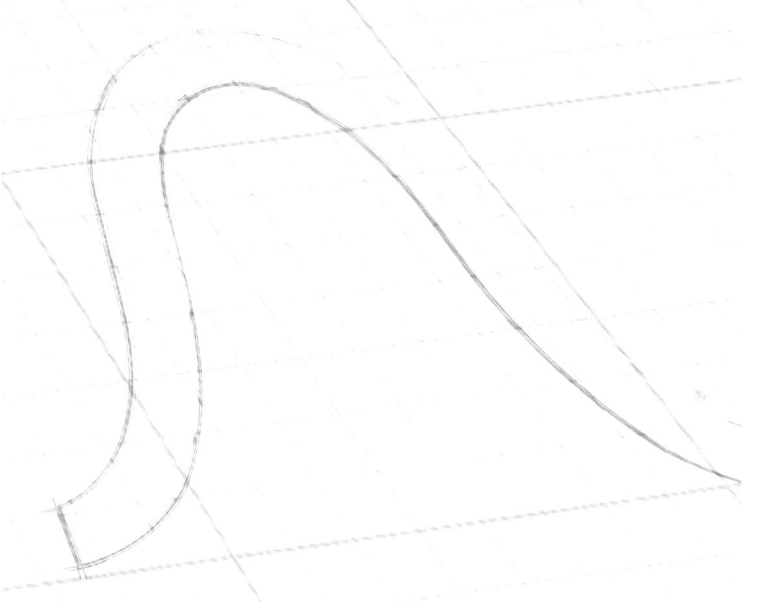

Dr. Paul Hersey
with Diana Newton

Leadership Blueprint: Why We Better Lead and Lead Better
is published by:
Leadership Studies, Inc.
120 Preston Executive Drive, Ste. 101
Cary, NC 27513
(800) 330-2840

Copyright © 2012, Leadership Studies, Inc.
All rights reserved.

Printed in the United States of America
Leadership Studies, Inc. © 2012

ISBN 978-0-615-61810-4

This book is dedicated to the individual contributors, managers and executives around the globe that I have had the privilege of working with, learning from and watching develop over the last 50-plus years.

FOREWORD

Learning From the Master

I have had the opportunity to know many of the world's greatest leadership thinkers. It has been my honor to learn from brilliant teachers such as Peter Drucker, Richard Beckhard, Frances Hesselbein and Jim Kouzes. None have influenced my life and work as much as Dr. Paul Hersey. He is an amazing man and a wonderful teacher. In reading this book, you have been given the opportunity to learn from the master. Please take full advantage of this privilege.

Paul Hersey literally made my career. When I was a young Ph.D. student at UCLA, he was kind enough to let me follow him around, watch him teach and help him with his consulting clients. He gave me an education that money could not buy. He gave me the opportunity to be in the field of leadership development. Whatever I have accomplished in life is largely due to what I learned from Dr. Hersey.

The first time I saw Paul teach a course for senior leaders, I realized that he was in a class by himself. Several factors make Dr. Hersey stand out:

- Applicability: Paul is not interested in "theory for theory's sake." Leaders can immediately put his concepts to work on the job – and see the impact of his ideas on the people that they lead.
- Clarity: He taught me the value of using "nickel words" that his students could actually understand and use as

opposed to academic jargon that was intended to impress more than educate.
- Excitement: Before I met Paul, I didn't realize that learning could actually be fun. He has as wonderful sense of humor and has never lost his sense of excitement and adventure. His positive spirit about his work is contagious.
- Integration: Dr. Hersey is able to integrate ideas from widely diverse sources and combine them to form an integrated model for leadership that has never been matched. He is not only an expert on management, he is a philosopher on life.
- Value: What Paul teaches actually works. His concepts have been tested and proven valid by millions of leaders across the globe. His ideas are universal; they apply in every country and in every era. If leaders exist a thousand years from today, I am sure that they will still be using his concepts.

In reading this book, please realize that you are going to be going to both graduate school and trade school. Consider your reading to be graduate school because you will be learning from a teacher who has taught many of the greatest leaders and greatest thinkers in the world. Consider your reading to be trade school because you will be learning from a teacher who is sharing ideas that you can immediately apply in your life – both at work and at home.

Paul has always worked to make a positive difference in the lives of the people that he touches. If you apply what you learn from him, you will not only have a better life, you will be able to help countless other people have better lives. This is Dr. Paul Hersey's legacy.

Marshall Goldsmith was recently recognized as the world's most influential leadership thinker in the bi-annual "Thinkers50" study sponsored by the *Harvard Business Review*. His 31 books include the *New York Times* bestsellers, "MOJO" and "What Got You Here Won't Get You There."

TABLE OF CONTENTS

Leadership: Looking Back and Going Forward 11

Situational Leadership®: Common Sense, Organized 23

Leading at the Speed of Light 35

The Language of Leadership 49

Got Talent? 65

Keep Them Going — and Growing 79

Out of the Darkness and Into the Light 97

CHAPTER ONE

LEADERSHIP: LOOKING BACK AND GOING FORWARD

You may know that I have spent much of my professional lifetime – over 58 years, in fact – standing in front of people and explaining my thoughts about leadership. So, you may wonder what I have left to say on the subject after teaching and consulting all over the world for so long. Well, my answer is, "Plenty!"

I am in my 80s now and well aware that it is time to say what I still have to say. I hope you will read on, and more importantly, take action as the leader that you are and can become. As one of the famous Delaney sisters, Bessie, said at age 103, "When you get real old, you lay it all on the table. There's an old saying: Only little children and old folks tell the truth. " I don't know about the truth, but I can let you in on my truth, based on decades of conversations with leaders.

While I have always felt passionate about developing leaders, I now feel an unsettling urgency. I believe we are in a global leadership crisis – a void of clarity about where to go and what to do that is unprecedented. It is a crisis that requires attention, resources and commitment on the part of individuals and organizations of all kinds. So, consider this book my howl from the rooftop, my megaphone to the masses:

"Listen up! Show up! Step up! We need good leaders – NOW!"

Leadership Through the Ages

People have long been interested in what makes a great leader. My own investigations about it resulted in Situational Leadership® – a behavior-based model woven from the "best of the best" historical thinking. Grounded in research and time-tested methodologies, the model has proven versatile and relevant by proving compatible with the models of today.

To put this in perspective, I'd like to start by putting leadership in historical context. This will be a high-level look at key developments that have shaped our views of leadership across thousands of years. Why? History lessons may be interesting in and of themselves, but it is even better if they are ***relevant*** to the challenges we face today in developing leaders. I believe that in looking at what has worked and what has not, what has endured and what has evaporated, there are lessons that can help leaders navigate the chaotic present and the future we cannot fully imagine. Simply put, if we look back over thousands of years, we may be able to see our way forward through the fog and respond with more than just good reaction time.

This timeline distills leadership through the ages down to its essence:

Leadership Through the Ages at a Glance

	Power Base	Followers	Era
Leaders **are born** with it	Physical Strength	Tribesmen	Pre-Civilization

	Power Base	Followers	Era
Leaders are born to do it	Birthright and Divine Right	Subjects	Middle Ages
Leaders rise to it	Traits of "Great Men"	Ordinary People	18th - 20th Century
Leaders command it	Control	Workers	18th - 20th Century
Leaders learn it	Influence	Anyone	Mid-20th Century

As we'll explore, leaders primarily used physical, religious and economic control to literally "rule the day" for centuries. It is not until the 20th century that we experience a break in that pattern, a fundamental discontinuity that results in new ways of leading. I'll tell you a bit more about each era in the rest of this chapter and in the chapters that follow as we look at the leadership dilemmas of today and tomorrow and ideas for how you can lead even better.

Primitive Might

Maybe I'm just feeling as "old as civilization," but I'd like to go considerably further back than I usually have in my research to our primitive ancestors. The stakes then were nothing less than survival against a host of predators and other environmental threats. How did a select few prevail and become tribal leaders when the choice was to kill or be killed? First, size and strength were an advantage. That physical might, coupled with a good defensive tool such as the club, fostered families and followers who looked to these leaders for protection and direction. A sharpened club became a spear, which could be used to hunt for not only food but to fight against other humans competing for it. Long-term power was based on survival skills. Failure to follow meant certain death. Leadership was primitive might aided by superior tools.

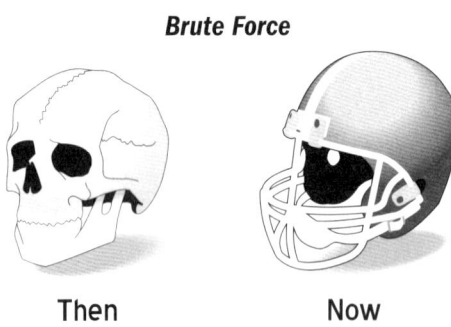

Brute Force

Then   Now

"Brute force" as a basis of leadership may have dawned in pre-civilization, but it has certainly endured. Today, we see it in our sports, physiology, politics and the stories we tell. Humans under threat still rely on a "fight-or-flight" response. Dictators continue to rise and be overthrown through force. Politicians regularly accuse each other of running "dirty" campaigns. We still see movie audiences and computer gamers rally around violent characters (just think of the Terminator or Rambo, Mortal Kombat's Rain or Angry Birds) who use more sophisticated tools to take out a threat – though it is more likely to be an alien or a criminal than a hungry lion. And, don't we see this often today in the way we respond to aggressive business competitors and their tools? Armies of litigators regularly wage war to defend our economic turf, and we regularly embrace and replace new techno tools in hopes of vanquishing our competition.

Back then, such brute force was directed toward others who threatened the well-being of the group. As tribes of hunter-gatherers developed, we would have seen a less hierarchical kind of leadership that encouraged cooperation while developing independent and resourceful members capable of specialized tasks, such as skinning game, cleaning fish, cooking, making tools and collecting fruits and seeds. A key role was that of the tribal shaman who provided spiritual leadership by communicating with spirit ancestors and enlisting their aid in supporting the needs of the tribe.

Thinking about those early societies and their leaders, I can imagine the basic elements of Situational Leadership® in play even then. When wolves encircled the camp, the chief would need to give decisive direction to tribesmen who were not able to otherwise defend themselves. Young warriors would learn to throw weapons, ride ponies and spot game under the supervision of more seasoned hunters. Those refusing to listen to the elders might be expelled from the group to try and survive on their own. More seasoned tribesmen might be included in a tribal council with the shaman, participating in important decisions and learning of the shaman's visions. Powerful hunters and warriors would have been fully empowered to kill.

Even then, depending on the situation, followers were likely to have experienced different leadership styles, though perhaps not from the same person.

> LEADERS HAVE BEEN USING DIFFERENT STYLES WITH PEOPLE DOING DIFFERENT TASKS FOR A VERY LONG TIME!

From Might to Divine Right

Tribal hunting and gathering led to domesticated livestock and agriculture. Large herds and flocks were fenced and tended by the first "ownership" societies, and people lived in denser, less transitory settlements. In these times, leaders tended to be those who accumulated the most land, had the best tools and supported the most people. Landowners became the social elite who provided for and directed those who worked the land and the animals.

With accumulated wealth, the social elite morphed into a ruling class during the Middle Ages. The different leadership styles used by the warrior and the shaman were essentially lost as fire gave way to fences for protection; the spear was supplanted by the scepter as a symbol of power; priests displaced shamans. In some societies, kings were given the same spiritual status as gods. In many eastern and western cultures, spiritual and asset power merged into the doctrine of the divine right of kings, which conferred absolute power to the monarch, whose authority was based on the will of God. To defy, depose or attempt to restrict the ruler was to challenge God and risk not only your life but your entire afterlife. Needless to say, most subjects were obedient! Democracy existed in comparatively few places, and participation by followers was often restricted to elite land-holding aristocrats.

Great Men

Given that individual, often charismatic, leaders had prevailed for centuries, we can see why 18th-century historian Thomas Carlyle declared, "The history of the world is but the biography of great men." Subsequently, scholars became interested in defining the essential character traits of leaders. Though they looked at Alexander the Great and Abraham Lincoln, Napoleon and Gandhi, Jesus Christ and Julius Caesar, researchers could not consistently identify common traits that guaranteed success among them.

Opponents of the "Great Men" theory of leadership immediately countered that leaders are products of their societies, their choices and opportunities shaped by their cultures. I believe this era is the pivot point for what we now know about effective leadership. The belief that, "leaders are born not made," began to quickly erode. Industrialization demanded lots of people in lots of leadership roles. They had to be chosen based on skill and will, on savvy and moxie.

Control by Captains of Industry

By the late 18th century, two key revolutions fundamentally challenged long-held ways of leading. The American Revolutionary War freed the colonies from British rule and created a functioning democracy in the fledgling United States. The steeply hierarchical rule of monarchs was toppled and ordinary citizens could participate in government through political office and voting. Advances in technology also powered the Industrial Revolution, during which many agrarian societies in Western cultures had to make room for the rapid expansion of manufacturing and a population explosion that could man production lines. A new source of great wealth grew from the ownership of factories and machinery.

Economic Might

We begin to see a proliferation of leadership roles, if not styles, in society. The prominent leaders in this era – railroad and shipping magnates and textile barons – were not from a single aristocratic class. Their backgrounds were quite diverse and, in many cases, humble. But, they seized the opportunity to invest in new technologies and were committed to mass production at minimal costs.

The profit motive placed a premium on efficiency and control of both processes and people. These new industrialists had little choice but to rely on factory foremen and mill supervisors to act as leaders with unrestrained, often misused, authority over the line workers. They were to keep order and meet production quotas. Workers were viewed as merely "hands" who were to follow directions and perform repetitive tasks quickly. Owners and shift leaders alike generally shared the belief that workers were inefficient, and if left to their own devices, would not perform at a satisfactory level. This assumption made it clear that not everyone could lead. Leaders lead; workers work. There was still a clear hierarchy of power and use of a directive, command-and-control leadership style was believed to be necessary.

Between You and Me: Leadership as Influence

But, the absolute power of management was checked as labor unions formed and gave workers an official voice about pay, benefits and working conditions in contract negotiations. For the first time, employees began "working with" instead of "working for" their leaders. We see the seeds of participative management take hold, as owners began to realize that an actively involved workforce is a more productive workforce.

From the 20th century forward, new "democratic" ways of leading began to be explored. Since the search for traits in "Great Men" had failed, a close look at behaviors – what leaders do with others in a particular situation and how it influences them – took center stage. After all, behavior is observable, empirical and measurable. If we could objectively record what effective leaders do, then others could watch and learn how to do it, right?

We entered new territory, overturning certain fundamental assumptions about leadership that had been held for thousands of years.

- If leadership is not just about me as an individual, then it must be **about others**.
- If leadership is not just about the person, then it **depends on the situation**.
- If leadership is not inborn, it **can be learned**.
- If leadership does not belong to one, it **can be exercised by many**.

CHAPTER ONE

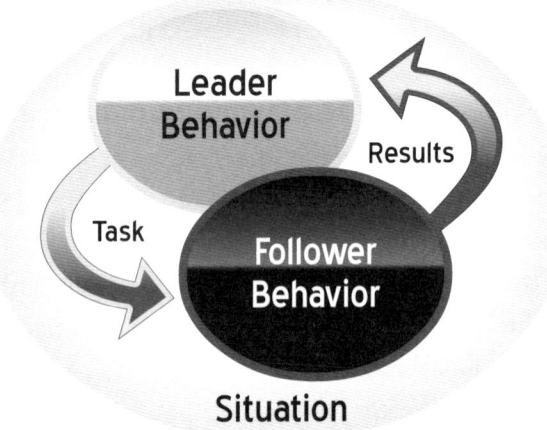

This interactive, interpersonal view of leader and follower, manager and employee informs organizational life today. And, in every organizational system, interactions between leaders and followers are occurring all day, every day. We live and work in a networked world that is more like an ecosystem than an organizational chart.

Of course, organizations would like to have a consistent, high-performing business universe that assures them of results. So, they continually seek out the newest leadership development theories and models: seven habits, four quadrants, three steps, the magic minute, and a partridge in a pear tree.

I have spent over 50 years of my life studying, teaching and weaving together the many profound, prolific and popular ideas about leadership that have circulated through our culture. I feel no need to repeat those findings here, as I have written numerous articles and books and delivered hundreds of workshops to make those connections.

It has taken thousands of years to move beyond a single individual, directive, command-and-control style of leadership. Leadership that provides the why, what and how is part of our societal DNA and transcends culture. Directive, command-and-control leadership is still absolutely useful in times of uncertainty, crisis or when the consequences are dire.

> LIKE IT OR NOT, DIRECTIVE LEADERSHIP IS DEEPLY FAMILIAR TO US. PARTICULARLY IN TIMES OF STRESS, WE TEND TO LOOK UP FOR ANSWERS, NOT WITHIN OR BETWEEN.

It is only recently that we came to understand that **learning** is a vital aspect of becoming a leader and being an effective one over time. Leadership today presents a very different picture than we began with: flatter organizations, 360-degree instantaneous communications and distance relationships. In this exponentially explosive Digital Information Age, we have had very few years of experience with distributed, shared, empowered, culturally literate leadership.

But, are the essentials so different? What works? You can drown in the literature, webcasts and blogs that espouse how to be an effective leader today. A quick Google search will confirm that assertion. The pendulum has swung from one way of leading to a thousand considerations. But, we have had to – and must continue to – diversify our views and our leadership practices to keep pace with the technology and global business trends.

We now understand that leadership is really focused on others and on outcomes. And, we now lead in deeply interconnected economic and culturally diverse contexts. Engagement has bottomed out, yet many stay because they feel like economic prisoners in their jobs. As our youngest generations join the workforce, they desperately seek a purpose they can believe in and few are finding it at the office. Turnover is rapid and high.

But, you not only make a difference, you make **the** difference. Research from the Gallup organization has revealed that the number one reason people leave a job is their leader. However, for those who are engaged, the number one reason they stay is also their leader. Your behavior, passion and choices have a tremendous influence on your people. And, influence is what leadership is all about in the 21st century.

Each chapter in this book will offer you a few key insights for you to hold onto while surfing the tsunami of change in which we live. So, read on. You will find that what the great warrior, the good king and the factory boss did should not be dismissed. Command-and-control (what we call a telling style) is still useful today – just not with everyone, everywhere, all the time. Nor is "servant leadership" with fully empowered employees (what we call a delegating style) the magic wand that will chase away our current woes. The way the tribal shaman led so long ago, now thematically revived by the reality TV show "Survivor" (what we call a participating style), works with some modern-day corporate employees too. One style does not fit all.

THERE IS NO ONE RIGHT WAY TO LEAD.
BUT, THERE IS ONE RIGHT WAY FOR <u>YOU</u> TO LEAD RIGHT <u>NOW</u>, RIGHT <u>WHERE YOU ARE</u>. YOU CAN <u>LEARN</u> HOW.

CHAPTER TWO

SITUATIONAL LEADERSHIP®: COMMON SENSE, ORGANIZED

The tweet. The text. The sound bite and the crawl. Calling all this "information overload" is an understatement at this point. To me, it feels like a continual peppering of buckshot to the brain. Much of it may be interesting, but the sheer volume has accelerated past the mind's ability to take it all in much less process it. But, I am finally wise enough — or at least old enough — to know that there is no going backwards. I also recognize that my grandkids' generation doesn't feel this way. Ironically, I have always considered myself someone who "cuts to the chase" and doesn't wrap ideas in a lot of lengthy, obscure, academic language. So, this chapter represents a compromise of sorts for me.

Consider this my "personal tweet" on leadership. It is longer than 144 characters but provides as succinct a description of why Situational Leadership® helps leaders make their worlds better, especially in these chaotic times. It is informed by the six decades I have spent observing leaders and evaluating the impact of their attempts to effectively influence their peers, their direct reports and their organizations for the better.

Why Has Situational Leadership® Withstood the Test of Time?

I have been asked this question in many ways and more times

than I can remember. So many leadership theories, books and principles have found their way into the limelight only to give way to the next big thing. Companies and individuals tend to chase the latest guru or book as if it will be a magic potion instead of staying with the tried and true and following through (more on this issue in Chapter 3). I understand the quest. I have been on a decades-long search for the latest and greatest magic driver to improve my golf game. Even so, Situational Leadership® has consistently turned out to be the most highly rated component of many leadership development programs for years.

When I boil it down, I can count on one hand the reasons why this model has endured and continues to provide "ah-ha's" to leaders from first-time supervisors to executives. These five characteristics have proven Situational Leadership® to be built to last. They are:

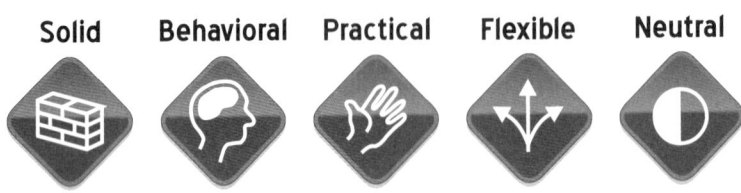

SITUATIONAL LEADERSHIP® HAS A SOLID FOUNDATION IN THE BEST THINKING ABOUT LEADERSHIP.

Reason #1: Situational Leadership® has a solid foundation. First and foremost, I believe Situational Leadership® has remained not only popular, but more importantly, relevant and practical for over 50 years because it has a **solid foundation**. It was born from the study and integration of a number of groundbreaking contributions in the field of leadership development that sought (and found) answers to questions like these:

- Is the *attitude or the personality* of the leader more important than his or her *behavior*?
- Is *participation* the best approach to leading others?
- How about *directive or empowering* approaches?
- What role should the *needs of the individual* play in the style of the leader?
- What (if any) impact does the *environment* play in the success of the leader?

Initially, I thought the results from these studies suggested incompatible answers to such questions, which was confusing. For instance, if a participative leadership approach was good because it demonstrated concern for both people and their results, then by default, a directive or empowering approach wouldn't be effective, right? Several of us focused on that confusion in an effort to make sense of it all, and hopefully, to provide an explanation that leaders would find useful. The product of that effort was Situational Leadership® which is a behavior-based model that thousands of leaders worldwide have utilized. Its lineage includes Maslow's hierarchy and McGregor's mindsets, the Johari window, the Managerial Grid and many more. We believe that it complements rather than contradicts any other leadership approach. So, let's be clear, Situational Leadership® would have never existed without the contributions of the thought leaders who came before it. The model is planted in rich soil.

SITUATIONAL LEADERSHIP® IS FOCUSED ON BEHAVIOR, NOT ATTITUDE OR MINDSET, POTENTIAL OR TALENT.

Reason #2: Situational Leadership® is all about observable behavior — in leaders and their people. When it comes to influencing others, mindset matters. Talent helps — so does a winning personality and executive hair. But, the fact is that unless you are a neurosurgeon, you cannot see what is going on inside someone's head. Leadership is about what you do with, for or to others. Your people can only see and experience your behavior, and believe me, they will decide whether you are an effective leader or not. What you think and feel may or may not be aligned with what you actually do. In my years of studying married couples with Carl Rogers, I have often heard one partner insist, "But I love her!" when describing an angry fight that took place. The tears tell the story that matters most. So, goal number one for any leader is to match up your mindset with your behavior.

Observable behavior is also measurable. Organizations today are highly metrics-driven. As my dear colleague Peter Drucker, one of the most influential writers about management practices, once said, "If you can't measure it, you can't manage it." Many of the people we have worked with seem daunted by their responsibility to evaluate the "soft skills" their people are supposed to demonstrate. After all, how can you measure things like influence, empathy and collaboration? How can your boss reliably measure your effectiveness at coaching, delegation or team building?

Too many people make too many measurements too complicated. Measurement is simply a way to observe something in order to reduce uncertainty. It is not always about finding absolute precision. This is particularly true in the realm of human interactions. It can help us confirm or course-correct when we consider key questions. Are we going in the right direction? How satisfied are our customers? How engaged are our employees?

Let's take coaching as an example. If I want to know how good a coach you are, I could shadow your coaching conversations and record how many times you gave specific task direction, how many times you asked an open-ended question or how often you proposed an alternative course of action. Of course, this is a pretty granular level of behavioral analysis that most managers have little, if any, time or opportunity to do. If we take it up a level, we could measure how many times you have used a particular coaching style and seen improvements as a result. That, too, would be behavior-based and measurable but far more practical and realistic. Situational Leadership® helps you understand which behaviors are related to four basic leadership styles and when each style will work best.

THEORY AND INSIGHT CAN GIVE YOU GREAT THINGS TO THINK ABOUT. SITUATIONAL LEADERSHIP® GIVES YOU PRACTICAL THINGS TO DO.

Reason #3: Gandhi once said, "A religion that takes no account of practical affairs and does not help to solve them is no religion." I can say the same about leadership theories. Situational Leadership® has endured because it is **practical** and useful in real life. While I hope it provides insight and inspiration, I know it does more than that. Our clients have told me time and again that the model is *simple to understand and easy to use*. Because leaders can quickly grasp it, they can take action rapidly and see a difference in results. And, this is as it should be. Any leadership model intended to provide its users with a road map to results should (at a minimum) give them the tools to begin their journey, as well as the confidence to believe they can complete it.

You, too, may have seen young knowledge workers move up and take on leadership roles. They may have done remarkable things with code but know little about leadership and are skeptical of human skills training. Time and again we have seen the Situational Leadership® template-driven approach to human behavior prove to be a revelation and an unbelievable comfort to these linear thinkers. It has been a joy to watch this dynamic transpire, particularly when leaders are confronted with situations they have yet to experience.

You see, people managers need technical, human and conceptual skills. Robert Katz had it right when he noted that these three skill sets show up at every level, but how much time we spend using each skill changes at each level of the organization. Proportionately less technical skill is needed as an individual advances from lower to higher levels in the organization but more conceptual skill is necessary.

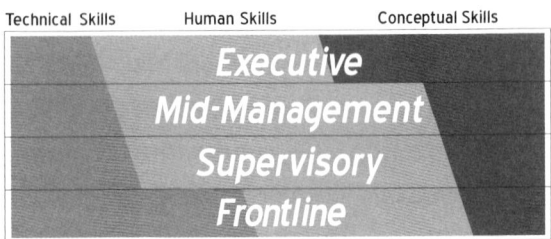

SITUATIONAL LEADERSHIP®: COMMON SENSE, ORGANIZED | 29

Supervisors at lower levels need considerable technical skill because they are often required to train and develop technicians and other employees in their sections. At the other extreme, executives in a business organization do not need to know how to perform all the specific tasks at the operational level. However, they should be able to see how all these functions are interrelated in accomplishing the goals of the total organization. This ability is particularly important because the executives' focus at the higher organizational levels is increasingly more external and global.

But, the need for human skills runs the gamut of your leadership life. We've constructed the Situational Leadership® Model to improve your ability across the following four core (and highly interdependent) competencies that will go the distance with you. I despise false promises, so trust me on this. If you can do these things, your relationships with your people and their results will get better.

DIAGNOSE	ADAPT	COMMUNICATE	ADVANCE
Understand the situation and how it needs to change.	Formulate an approach based on the diagnosis.	Implement the approach in a manner that people can both understand and accept.	Move yourself and your people in a direction of continuous improvement.

SITUATIONAL LEADERSHIP® BUILDS LEADERSHIP "FITNESS"— STRENGTH, FLEXIBILITY AND ENDURANCE.

Reason #4: The "big four" competencies will build your leadership muscles. Chapter 3 will address endurance. Now, let's talk about flexibility – both in your current role and across other levels of leadership you may take on. In Situational Leadership® we begin by talking a lot about the importance of accurate diagnosis (Performance Readiness® for a specific task) and adapting your leadership style to match. If you can learn to do that (and I know you can), you will have a flexible navigation system for getting things done through others. Just like a GPS, you will have options (Fastest route? Most use of highways?) but they will center on which leadership style to use. You will never be lost again (unless you don't look and listen) because, as the leader, you use the model within your own frame of reference. What is the knowledge needed for that task? What interest and motivation am I looking for as I assign this project? It is instantaneously personalized, customizable and not overly prescriptive. Situational Leadership® allows people to respond in the moment: right here, right now.

One of the biggest problems for leaders is (over)relying on just one leadership style, usually a very comfortable one. Perhaps you've heard the saying, "You can't win at golf with only one club in your bag." Well, here's a story of how Situational Leadership® can help you get out of that trap.

One of our clients had an influx of new hires. He felt this new group had enough capability to learn quickly and be productive from their hire date (first mistake: wrong diagnosis). Once he recognized some initial floundering, he adapted his style to provide the initial guidance and training needed instead of frustrating them by under-leading. The result? Turnover was reduced within the first 60 days.

As I said in the first chapter, all of us can and should exercise leadership. The four competencies I just identified are needed each and every day, whether you are in the role of:

- **PERSONAL LEADER**: No direct reports or formal authority but need to influence laterally and upward
- **TEAM LEADER**: A manager or supervisor with formal responsibility for any number of individual contributors
- **ORGANIZATIONAL LEADER**: A director or manager of other managers with formal responsibility for a region, division or business unit

Additionally, the role of the leader is by no means confined to formal organizational life. Parents can clearly implement across these competencies as well. I have heard some of the most "relief-ridden" success stories from parents who recognized that Situational Leadership® is flexible enough to help them in their role as family leader too.

 SITUATIONAL LEADERSHIP® IS THE SWITZERLAND OF LEADERSHIP MODELS.

Reason #5: The final reason I believe Situational Leadership® has withstood the test of time is that it is **neutral with regard to both values and culture.** From the values perspective, leaders can diagnose, adapt, communicate and advance for the express purpose of:

- Reorganizing a company or business unit
- Streamlining a delivery process

- Developing a drug that cures cancer
- Building a jet engine
- Robbing a bank

The values reside in the user, not in the model. Of course, this contributes to its flexibility as well.

As it applies to culture, I have helped leaders effectively apply Situational Leadership® on every continent but Antarctica and more countries than I've bothered to count since the late 1960s. With that as background, allow me to confirm the obvious; culture does in fact impact the process of leadership. Leader behavior delivered in New York City will look and feel different than the same leadership style delivered in Smoot, Wyoming or Siler City, North Carolina. The same is true if you compare styles delivered in China with styles delivered in Spain, Germany or Brazil. For example, the level of challenge and debate you would witness within a participative leadership style in Italy is far more than you would see in Japan. What we call the "telling" style might take longer in India than in Denmark.

But, like values, the specifics of a culture only matter to the model's users. They are the ones who swim in it. Situational Leadership® is neutral and inclusive enough to point out that whether you are swimming in the Pacific or the Mediterranean, the Indian Ocean or Lake Michigan, you will need to consider your breathing and your stroke.

The ability of the model to transcend cultural differences is of key importance, as globalization requires leaders to work across countries and languages and to honor local practices. As I see it, the essence of what successful and effective leaders do may be expressed differently from setting to setting. But, no matter where you are, people will need and respond to appropriate levels of direction and support, which will forever be a function of what they are being asked to accomplish.

CHAPTER THREE

LEADING AT THE SPEED OF LIGHT

There is a lot of buzz in the business world about global leadership — as if it is something new. It is not. From Julius Caesar to J.P. Morgan, from Marco Polo to Mark Zuckerburg, the desire to access and dominate new global markets is centuries old. Once there was a fairly simple (though brutal) equation that could result in expansion: take unquenchable ambition, send in strong armies, add plenty of resources and as much time as it takes and you add new territory to your empire.

The current equation for success is more like calculus than simple addition. Here's what I mean. First, picture yourself as one of Caesar's generals. Your mission? World domination. The diversity of your workforce? Zero (young male Roman citizen-soldiers speaking one language). Means of communication between units? One (human messenger). Time it takes for messenger communication to travel from Rome to Alexandria: two hours by chariot, then six days by sea.

Now, remove your laurel wreath. Imagine, instead, being Larry Page, one of the co-founders of Google and current CEO. Your mission? Facilitate access to information for the entire world and in every language (over 60 countries and 130 languages so far). Diversity of your workforce? Twenty-thousand men and women spanning five generations working in 76 different offices in 43 different countries. Means of communication between work units? Virtually through webcast, teleconference, cell phone, email, instant message, texts and tweets. Time it takes for an IM to travel from the Milan office to the data center in Oregon? An instant. Relief felt when cyber attacks from China are averted? Priceless.

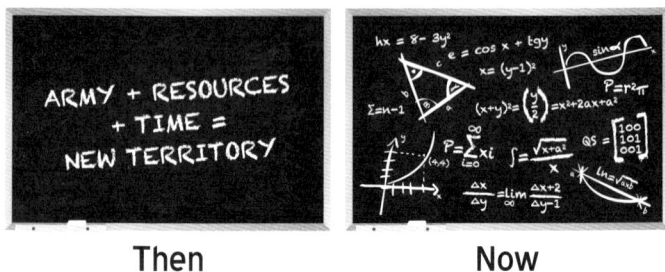

Then   Now

Critical Variables for Leaders Today

Today, global leadership is exponentially more challenging. Why? Because of these three critical variables:

- The **complex context** in which leaders must lead
- The **competencies** leaders need to succeed in that context
- The **consequences** of leadership actions are rapid, visible, but often unpredictable

As a leader today, you too are navigating a dizzying competitive landscape. You must be able to think strategically about opportunities that span continents and time zones. You need to develop nimble organizations that can innovate and respond at light speed. You must explore emerging markets to realize growth. You need to be culturally sensitive, flatten the organization, trim the fat and tweet what is happening from interaction to interaction. You are expected to be available and responsive 24/7.

The consequences of a poor strategy, slow response time, failure to adapt or a disengaged workforce can have painful, far-reaching consequences very quickly. Mainstay companies that unassailably dominated their markets for a hundred years, such as Sears and Kodak, are now fighting for survival. We all know that banking industry leaders engaged in mortgage practices that imploded in 2008, leading to a cataclysmic, overnight death spiral for several financial giants. World economies are still recovering from that collective failure of leadership. There is no certainty.

I asserted in the first chapter of this book that we are in a global leadership crisis. Here is a sobering fact from the Corporate Leadership Council to back up my belief:

ONLY 18% OF GLOBAL LEADERS TODAY ARE ACHIEVING BOTH THEIR SHORT-TERM PERFORMANCE OBJECTIVES AND BUILDING THE FOUNDATION FOR LONG-TERM GROWTH.

So, Google leaders Larry Page and Sergey Brin are extreme outliers among those leaders attempting to swim faster than the sharks before the next tsunami these days.

But, there is no need for despair. Why?

WE ALREADY KNOW A LOT ABOUT WHICH COMPETENCIES ARE NEEDED TO EQUIP LEADERS FOR SUCCESS WITHIN THIS COMPLEX CONTEXT. THAT IS NOT THE PROBLEM.

Google's People Analytics team released their findings on the "Eight Habits of Highly Effective Google Managers" last year. Needless to say, there was a lot of interest in what they concluded, which was met with lots of media and business attention. Frankly, I was amused. These "newly discovered" eight habits are great habits, but they are far from new and far from unique. My team and I at the Center for Leadership Studies, and many others in this field, have been training and consulting based on these competencies — and more that we've identified as critical — all over the world for decades.

What Google Just Figured Out		What We've Known and Taught for a While
Be a good coach.	1	"People skills" matter!
Empower your team and don't micromanage.	2	Empowerment works; so does participation and guidance.
Express interest in the team's success and personal well-being.	3	Success (outcomes) are short-lived in the absence of effectiveness (retention and high morale).
Don't be a sissy: Be productive and results-oriented.	4	Leaders add value by holding people accountable for measurable results.
Be a good communicator and listen to your team.	5	People need to "know you care" before they will "care what you know."
Help your employees with career development.	6	People are either moving forward or backward. Nothing stays the same.
Have a clear vision and strategy for the team.	7	If you don't know where you are going, it simply doesn't matter which path you choose.
Have key technical skills so you can help your team.	8	"Expert power" is a key driver of influence potential.

Adapted from: Google's Rules. *New York Times*. March 13, 2011.

Google's findings do remind me that new leaders and young, fast-growing companies have to discover long-standing leadership fundamentals ***for themselves***. And, judging by their business results, Google managers have clearly taken them to heart!

Knowing which competencies matter most is not the problem. Many leaders and organizations have offered training on coaching, communication, collaboration and more. Yet, many leaders and organizations are still not very good at doing these things. Why? Investing the necessary time, energy and resources ***over time*** to build and sustain core leadership skills is the root problem. Here's what tends to go wrong. Companies provide training courses on important competencies. Existing and aspiring leaders attend them. End of story.

> **SEEING LEARNING AS AN EVENT IS A MINDSET MISTAKE. REAL LEARNING IS A CONTINUOUS JOURNEY THAT REQUIRES PREPARATION AND FOLLOW-THROUGH.**

What we at The Center for Leadership Studies have known for a long time is that, becoming a leader is a journey — and not a series of workshops to be checked off the list — is a mindset must for both learners and companies. There is a proven formula that helps learning last:

- **Set expectations**: What will I learn and what difference will it make at work?
- **Learn**: Attend a training program, take an online course or listen to a podcast.
- **Practice on the job**: Try out your skills in your real-world business context.
- **Get feedback and support**: From your manager, your mentor or your chat buddy.

> "WHAT'S IN IT FOR ME?"
> MUST BE CLEAR ON THE FRONT END.
> WE CALL IT **LEARNER READINESS**.

> "HOW AM I DOING?"
> MUST BE REINFORCED ON THE BACK END.
> WE CALL IT **LEARNING TRANSFER**.

The front end and the back end of the learning journey — three out of four essential parts — are often missing or poorly executed. So, the skill-building effort becomes a house of cards that collapses quickly. Leaders depart the workshop, module or webcast and resume doing their frantic tasks and interacting with others in much the same way as they did the day before. What was learned never gets transferred to the workplace. Yet, by securing executive sponsorship, engaging managers and encouraging peer support, companies can create a learning culture that **increases learning transfer by more than 90%**! We build our offerings off of a validated leadership competency model, focusing on behavior change, and building in touch points pre, during and post training to ensure sustainment of learning and true behavioral change back on the job.

Let's go back to Google's "Eight Habits" list. It is also organized in priority order of importance for which they are also to be commended. If coaching is among the most important leadership skills for new people managers and team leaders to learn — and it is — learn how to coach early on. Certainly Larry and Sergey's skills in strategic planning, change management and building bench strength in the organization are mission critical at this point. But, they didn't start with 20,000 employees. Google started with just the two of them. These future global leaders needed to develop their **personal leadership skills first**. They needed to be able to collaborate effectively, demonstrate basic business acumen and negotiate with vendors before they made a single hire. As the company grew, they would have acted as and managed other team leaders. Now they would need to manage performance and develop others.

FIRST THINGS FIRST: THE SEQUENCE OF LEARNING AND DEVELOPING SKILLS MATTERS.

The sequence of learning I endorse is based on the premise that personal leadership is the foundation on which you build team leadership, which can then prepare you for organizational leadership. Senior leaders will need all of the "lower level" leadership skills and then some in order to be effective. For example, we would expect you to draw on your **personal** resilience in order to help your **team** leaders address resistance to a significant change process for which you are the **organizational** change sponsor. Every rookie in the minor leagues needs to do a lot of batting practice before going to the majors. But, not every hitter "in the show" lives up to his million-dollar contract. (I'll address more about senior leaders who derail in Chapter 7, The Shadow of the Leader).

Leadership in the Headlights

Remember the 2010 heroic incident of the 33 Chilean miners who were trapped underground and survived for 69 days before being rescued? The personal and team leadership demonstrated in that remarkable situation has been well documented. The foreman, Luis Urzua who took charge, set up careful food rationing, digging for groundwater and siphoning water from machine radiators. He organized the space into work areas, such as a makeshift gym and sleeping quarters. He kept the men on a regular schedule by shining the headlights of trucks in the mine to simulate daylight. His final order was that he would be the last one lifted to the surface during their rescue.

Meanwhile, up above, we saw two very different responses from the highest-level leaders. Chile's President Sebastian Pinera inspired the nation to keep hopeful vigil while the private mining company declared that it not only could not pay to rescue the miners, it could not even pay their wages.

But I Don't Have Time

With the rapid changes in our technologies today, it is hard to keep up with all the information coming at us. Telephones, texts and tweets can all sound off at the same time, seducing us away from what we most need to be doing. Research shows that in

2010, the average business employee sent and received about 110 email messages daily. Some estimates suggest that workers are spending up to half their day on email! Most executives' calendars are booked for weeks on end, making it difficult to identify open dates to attend training, much less to be involved in the follow-up support needed to make learning "stick" for others. What leader, at any level, has the time to commit to ongoing leadership development activities?

Here is where I am going to make a bold, but unequivocal assertion:

UNLESS LEADERS DEVELOP THEMSELVES AND THEIR PEOPLE, THEY WILL NEVER ACHIEVE DESIRED BUSINESS RESULTS.

Too many people think that leadership development is somehow separate from or less important than achieving business goals. Investing in the "people factor" is regarded as nice rather than necessary, discretionary instead of business critical. We see this time and again when budgets are cut: learning and development takes a hit at the very time companies need effective leadership the most. I believe this is a false dichotomy, and more importantly, a bad business move!

Let me offer some rational data to back up my assertion. In the following bar graph, we see that great people managers not only improve employee performance but also emotional commitment (engagement) and intent to stay (retention) by double digits! What company wouldn't be exhilarated by such results? In light of this, how can anyone make a credible business case against developing great people leaders?

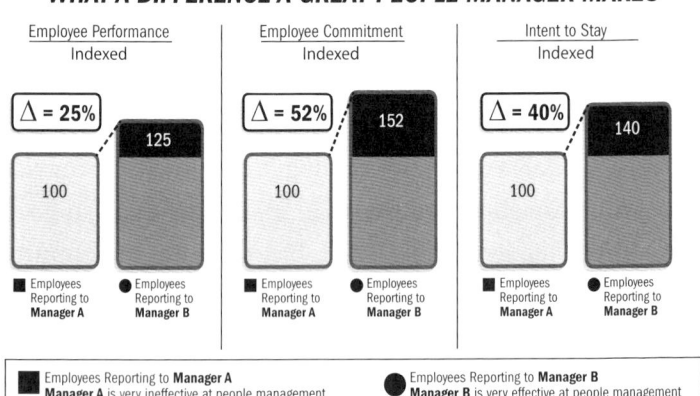

Unfortunately, first-time managers are more likely to hinder than enhance employee performance and potential; 60% of first-time managers underperform in their role.

Source: Learning and Development Roundtable. 2007. *Frontline Management Survey: Learning and Development Roundtable research.*

Efficiency is Part of the Leadership Lexicon

From our years of experience with clients from many industries, we know that Situational Leadership® is a framework for highly effective performance communication. But, it is also ***efficient*** performance communication. The more you can develop people who are highly committed, results-oriented and can work autonomously, the more it expands your scope. It enables both you and your people to have more time to focus on what you need to be doing: increasing performance and productivity, investing energy in creativity and innovation and preserving opportunities for research, reflection and critical thinking. And, if you teach your people to communicate back to you what you need to know, that enables you to better influence up and laterally and to better understand what is going on in other parts of the organization.

> **SITUATIONAL LEADERSHIP®
> IS EFFICIENT PERFORMANCE COMMUNICATION
> THAT CAN EXPAND YOUR SCOPE, TIME AND
> INFLUENCE CAPABILITY.**

I began this chapter talking about the complex context, competencies and consequences of global leadership today. A comprehensive 2011 study by the Corporate Leadership Council has drawn a detailed profile of the "great global leader" that includes an examination of personal background, aspirations, competencies and activities. We *were not* surprised to find that intercultural skills are important. We *were* surprised to find that many high-potential employees do not want global roles, and that many actual global leaders do not want to relocate. While there were a number of fascinating findings, none were more significant than this:

> **INFLUENCE IS THE MOST IMPORTANT
> COMPETENCY FOR GLOBAL LEADERS — AND ALSO
> THE ONE AT WHICH THEY ARE THE WORST.**

Only 25% of global leaders were effective at influence, which placed dead last among the 21 competencies measured. So, we have a lot of work to do to build great global leaders in just that one competency. We believe that influence is a fundamental personal leadership skill that should be developed and honed among "High Potentials" (HiPos) and executives alike. Given that global leaders are more likely to have responsibilities over individuals and teams with whom they lack direct authority, as well as more distance interactions, a repertoire of influence skills needs to be unpacked for the journey.

Remember the once popular phrase, "Think globally, act locally?" I still see it occasionally on bumper stickers here and there. It was originally used to raise awareness of the need to protect the environment. Now we "go green" instead.

Well, I'd like to resurrect excitement about that idea — with leadership in mind instead. Situational Leadership® is a model that marries the development of a global perspective with a plan for taking action right where you live. It is at the heart of our core competency of adapting. Just imagine a high-potential leader who has spent time learning a range of power and influence strategies, examined his or her own influence style and practiced cross-cultural communication before being asked to identify gaps in operational consistency and execution across geographies. The probability of his or her effectiveness would be much greater when discussing the issues with global peers and customers.

A Delicate Balance

Since change is now our constant, chaos-inducing companion, leaders need to become skilled tightrope walkers. Like Philippe Petit, who surreptitiously mobilized a team to run a wire between the Twin Towers of the World Trade Centers in 1974, planning and exquisite balance allowed him to survive while police and onlookers watched breathlessly as he promenaded between the buildings. For leaders today, the high-wire challenge is to balance the highly contradictory demands for lean efficiency with gymnastic flexibility. The problem is that the policies and procedures that ensure reliability and predictability in organizations tend to improve efficiency, but they reduce flexibility, responsiveness and time to market.

As I have said for years, "You can't balance very long on a stool with one or two legs." One of the reasons our clients have found Situational Leadership® so valuable is that it provides both high predictability and high adaptability. The model's integration of task and relationship keeps business outcomes and the people who drive them constantly integrated. The dance of diagnosing and adapting is dynamic, encouraging flexibility but also providing a measure of predictability. We know that change initiatives bring uncertainty, lower readiness to perform and loss of productivity with them.

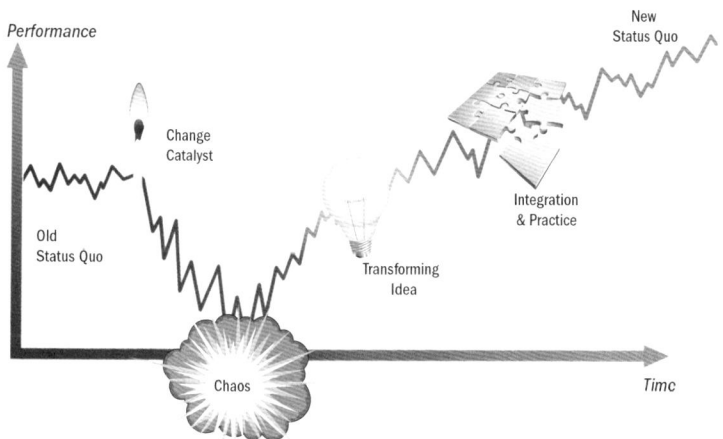

> *THE GOAL DURING CHANGE IS TO SHORTEN THE LENGTH AND IMPROVE DISCRETIONARY PERFORMANCE DURING THE INEVITABLE PERIOD OF CHAOS.*

Situational Leadership® gives you a crystal ball to do just that. Our change competencies help you proactively lead and manage change by equipping you to:

Diagnose
- Assess the readiness of individuals and the organization to make the change.

Adapt
- Anticipate how to shift your leadership style to provide the direction and support people are going to need.

Communicate
- Plan how you are going to communicate a clear, credible and convincing need for the change.

Advance
- Develop resilience in others for managing change.

That's as good as it is going to get on the high wire. Leaders must be change agents who create conditions for problem solving and innovation within reasonable boundaries of risk. Nothing less than organizational survival depends on it.

CHAPTER FOUR

THE LANGUAGE OF LEADERSHIP

Why are discussions of mission and vision so central to starting a business, formulating strategy or charting a new product line? Would you be surprised if my answer was, "Take another look at Alexander the Great and how he united his empire?"

You see, one of the reasons that Alexander the Great was *so great* is that he recognized the need for a lingua franca — a common language to be used by speakers of different languages. Alexander brought ancient Greek into usage not only to drive his military conquests but also to facilitate commerce, diplomacy, education and governance across three continents amongst speakers of hundreds of different tongues from the Mediterranean to Persia. This vast international network was united by a common Greek language and culture, while the king himself adopted foreign customs in order to rule his millions of ethnically diverse subjects.

Using Greek as the language of civilization was a very intentional strategy meant to help achieve his goal to "Hellenize" the European and Asian cultures in his empire. By doing so, Alexander both fueled the rapid expansion of his rule and ensured that new territories were consolidated as he moved forward.

CHAPTER FOUR

> **LEADERS UNIFY PEOPLE BY INTRODUCING A COMPELLING VISION AND CREATING A COMMON LANGUAGE.**

Alexander the Great's story demonstrates how powerful it can be when everyone is "on the same page." In a business setting today, we would say that his story is a powerful case study of alignment around a mission and vision that was driven by a change initiative. Now, if you've spent a single day in a current organization of almost any size, you've heard these highlighted terms.

- **Alignment**: Moving in the same direction (people understanding and agreeing with what they are doing and why)
- **Mission**: Building a new empire (making record profits for shareholders)
- **Vision**: Being first to unite cultures across three continents (being the industry leader)
- **Change Initiative**: Introducing and reinforcing Greek as the language across the entire enterprise (implementing a necessary new strategy)

In this chapter we will look at how we can communicate as leaders to unify our people around purpose, performance and place:

- The language of leadership
- Talking about performance and development
- Business communication across cultures

First, Beware the Entire Buzz

Mission, vision, alignment, change initiative: these and many other words and phrases are part of the lexicon of life in organizations. None of us are strangers to jargon. We know that different professions and industries have developed their own characteristic vocabularies — a kind of insiders' shorthand. You may have probably heard "artspeak" at a gallery opening in which the artist or critic inevitably spoke of "juxtaposed images." Or, you've had an unfortunate run-in with legalese — that tangled verbal jungle in which phrases like "pursuant to," "herein" and "in accordance with" confirm that you are in big trouble. Communications from the federal government have become such a barrier to understanding that "plain language" guidelines have been created to help us poor consumers have a clue.

When the language we typically use begins to cloak rather than clarify, to obscure rather than enhance shared understanding, we've got a problem. And, increasingly, the language of business has a problem. Consider the fact that a 2011 Harvard Business Review blog post, titled "I Don't Understand What Anyone Is Saying Anymore," broke a record for the most comments of all time and some server traffic records as well. It was all about the proliferation of increasingly meaningless business "buzz words." Comedian Stephen Colbert highlighted this trend when he coined the satirical term "truthiness" to point out how many leaders were making decisions "from the gut" without regard for the facts.

CHAPTER FOUR

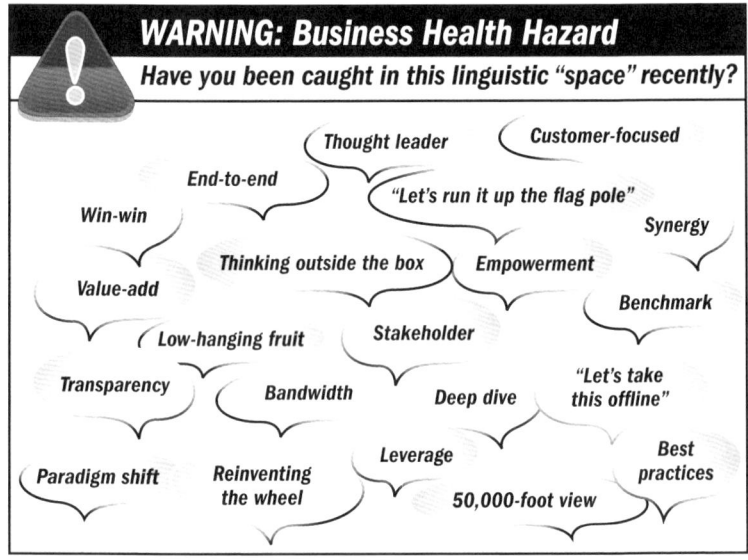

Once certain words or phrases enter the buzzword "space," they no longer have meaning that matters. They become, instead, the stuff of jokes and a likely indicator of mistrust and skepticism. Too often they are an unacknowledged gauge of organizational health and authenticity. For better or worse, there is a correlation between our language and our lives at work. The continuum runs from clear and simple to sarcastic and disconnected.

	Influence	
The Words We Use		**The Way We Work**
Plain English	→	Clarity of Purpose
Specialized Jargon	→	Siloed, Internal Focus
Buzz Words	→	Superficial Engagement
Punch Lines	→	Skeptical Distance

The Keys to Effective Leadership Communication

So, what is the leader's role in communicating clearly about the business instead of perpetuating mere "buzziness?" There has been a lot written about the importance of what leaders do, not just what they say. I believe that what leaders say is vitally important, too. Your people are watching **and** listening. They are looking to find ways to believe you. The words you choose as a leader set the tone and shape the culture of your organization. They can either go forward to elevate your people or come back to haunt you.

We have identified five key aspects of leadership communication that leaders need to be aware of and test their messages for today.

We are hard-wired to:	Your communication must be:	So they will think and feel:
Look for truth	Credible	"I believe you."
Look for recognition	Caring	"You understand me."
Look for information	Concise	"I needed to know that."
Look for relevance	Convincing	"You know what matters."
Look for simplicity	Clear	"I get it."

Our work with leaders is based on helping them learn and practice these communication fundamentals to build trusting relationships. Learning how to ***communicate with credibility*** begins at the personal leadership level and only becomes more important as you exercise team and organizational leadership. Many politicians are masterful at choosing short, compelling phrases that summarize a key theme. Who can forget "Mission Accomplished" or "Yes We Can?" Inspiring? Yes. Credible? No. The simple truth is that saying it doesn't make it so. Your people are looking for a history of consistency in which you "walk your talk."

Research shows that people's perceptions of your credibility are based on these factors:
- 50% empathy and caring
- 20% honesty
- 15% competence
- 15% commitment

You can see from these data that if people believe you care about them and the purpose you share, and are honest about what is happening, you are in the leadership zone. My colleagues Jim Kouzes and Barry Posner have written extensively about how you can gain and lose credibility. Here is their bottom line: "Leadership is a relationship. You can't talk about leadership without talking about the expectations of those who are led. Simply put, people won't believe the message if they don't believe in the messenger."

> **TOO MANY LEADERS FALL INTO THE TRAP OF FAILING TO FRAME THE ISSUE OR PROBLEM FROM THEIR PERSPECTIVE.**

Take the story of what one COO learned when he became an "Undercover Boss" in the network TV series of the same name.

What a Waste

Larry O'Donnell, the COO of Waste Management, posed as a new employee for one week within his own giant company. He did a variety of jobs, from working the line in a recycling plant to riding on a garbage collection truck. His goal? To see what it was really like to do some of their most challenging jobs and to see how well communication between managers and frontline employees was going.

Larry, himself, had instituted a policy to improve productivity. Supervisors were supposed to observe at times to see that the garbage collection routes were intelligently designed, the number of stops was achievable and that customer service was good. But, he quickly saw that supervisors had misinterpreted the policy and made it punitive, discouraging any flexibility about stops. As a result, drivers felt spied upon by "guys in pickup trucks watching them" from down the street and felt so badgered about productivity that some female drivers were often not making enough restroom stops!

As a result, Larry learned that the policy was actually frustrating drivers and kept them from feeling free to really connect with the customers on their route. As communication traveled from the executive level down to frontline implementation, it had certainly gone off the rails! At least Larry found out and had a chance to fix the problem.

Sound familiar? Let's hope you don't have to go undercover to learn how your communications are received, implemented and experienced. You must anticipate expectations and reactions when crafting your communication. What information might be challenging to comprehend? What might cause a strong emotional reaction?

The quality of caring and empathy has too often been dismissed as "unprofessional" or minimized as too "touchy-feely." Over the years, I have said to many leaders in my classes, "Emotions are data too!" Reuven Bar-On, an authority on Emotional Intelligence (EQ), has noted that leaders with empathy can pick up subtle emotional signals that allow them to sense the unspoken emotions in a person or group. The cutting glance towards someone, the knit brow, the loaded silence — all provide information that attuned leaders can then access and explore. If you have any doubt that communicating with empathy has an influence on your job performance, look at just two key findings from a large-scale research study (data from 6,731 managers from 38 countries):

> **EMPATHY IS POSITIVELY RELATED TO JOB PERFORMANCE. _HAVING_ EMPATHY IS NOT THE SAME AS _SHOWING_ EMPATHY.**

Perceptions of credibility and caring often go hand-in-hand. For example, Southwest Airlines is known for being an airline with "heart." How many companies do you know that use adjectives like "warmth" and "friendliness" in their mission statement? The company's reputation for caring can be seen in the following story that went viral on the Internet.

> **Worth the Wait**
>
> Mark Dickinson was trying to catch a flight in an effort to see his dying grandson. Desperate to make the trip and find his grandson still alive, he had asked to move further up in a long, slow-moving security line but was having little luck.
>
> Mark's wife, Nancy, decided to call the airline to see if there was any way Southwest could hold the flight.
>
> As Mark finally rushed to the gate, the pilot of his plane said, "Are you Mark? We held the plane for you and we're so sorry about your grandson."
>
> Regaining his breath, Mark said, "I can't thank you enough for this."
>
> The pilot responded with this assurance, "They can't go anywhere without me and I wasn't going anywhere without you. Now relax. We'll get you there. And again, I'm so sorry."

By committing just 12 minutes to wait for Mark and offering a few caring words, the pilot won a family's gratitude forever and gained the airline priceless positive PR as a bonus. His decision and message integrated all five aspects of effective leadership communication in a momentary exchange.

Of course, getting people to slow down and wait is not the problem many leaders have. Instead, they spend a lot of energy trying to convince people to hurry up and get on board with their ideas for change. Now the conventional leadership approach is to try and persuade people to do something different by giving them reasons why they should change their minds.

USING RATIONAL REASONS TO CONVINCE PEOPLE LOOKS LIKE THIS:

Define problem ▸ Analyze problem ▸ Recommend solution

But, many psychological studies have shown that when people believe something strongly, their immediate reaction to information that indicates otherwise is to assume that something must be wrong with the source.

Instead, effective leaders who need to be persuasive use a fundamentally different approach from the linear, rational one. They communicate by first getting attention, then stimulating desire and only then reinforcing with reasons.

INSPIRING BUY-IN, ENTHUSIASM AND ACTION LOOKS LIKE THIS:

Get attention ▸ Stimulate desire ▸ Reinforce with reasons

One-time communications are rarely convincing so as implementation proceeds, you'll need to stay in communication with your people, modify your message as things evolve, and continue what is now a conversation instead of just an announcement.

Knowing that we are all time challenged, it is also important for leaders like you to whittle away your words, killing any fluff and all the buzz until just the "headline" is left. By "headline" I mean the big message that can't be missed, is clear and concise and comes first. Difficult or important messages wrapped in lots of words only make people impatient since they have to sift to find what is really relevant.

Creating a Common Language of Performance

While leaders need to be effective communicators, they also need to build that same capability in their people and within the overall organization. Organizations need a lingua franca of their own. They need it to bridge different functional areas and they need it to bridge intercultural communication between global regions and external partners. Have you ever been in a meeting in which members of Corporate, Manufacturing, R&D and Sales and Marketing functions try problem solving and reaching consensus? Each has its own processes, acronyms and standards. From what I have seen and heard in some companies, it still sounds like the cross-dialects of 350 B.C.

We have found that when a performance language is learned, used and reinforced across company boundaries, the lingua franca effect takes hold. Imagine once again being in that same meeting with members of Manufacturing, R&D and Sales and Marketing. But, instead of cross talk, everyone is completely in sync when talking about performance. When we say a manager is really "committed" to a certain project, head nods of agreement indicate it is understood this person is motivated, is taking ownership and will do what it takes to get this project done and done well. People knowingly agree that a proposed SAP implementation will result in "regression." And further, those managers should be prepared to offer more "direction" in the implementation of the new process.

Using abbreviated codes such as "R3" or "S1" from the Situational Leadership® Model or a term like "regression" or "direction" is not jargon. Why? Because everyone at the table knows and understands what these mean — and would in any other meeting — regardless of function or geography. So, on the contrary; it becomes a remarkably efficient way to discuss performance. It joins people in a common, inclusive understanding that helps advance results and development of those doing the work. In fact, managers could then go back to the line or the lab or the field and contract with their people around Performance Readiness® and style because the employees get it too.

Here are just a few real-world examples of how a common language around performance and application of Situational Leadership® has contributed to positive results.

Situation	Problem	
Influx of new hires	Assumption that they could be productive right away	
New task delegated to experienced employee who was willing but not able	Leader was using one delegating style with everyone all the time	
Annual performance appraisals	Unclear picture of individual performance	
Relative performance calibration	Inconsistent evaluation and team accountability measures	

Even when we know the key terms and metrics, organizations and teams need to invest in checking for understanding. When managers need to evaluate performance, they must work to truly gain agreement about what they mean when comparing how "difficult" and "complex" their employees' work has been. Is it more "difficult" to collaborate effectively in an internal cross-functional team, or to elicit collaboration from different vendors in the supply chain that contribute to a product's success? Is it more "complex" to scale a project for implementation across multiple divisions or across multiple countries or both? While such discussions may take time, they are vitally important for consistency, fairness and in ultimately defining results in a meaningful way.

Change	Result
Shift in leadership style from under leading them to providing enough guidance and training	Reduced turnover within first 60 days
Leader recognized need to adapt style on case-by-case basis	Task completion; improved productivity and motivation; greater leader flexibility
Manager employed readiness assessment along with standard review template	Better recognition of strengths and development needs; richer discussion of stretch for upcoming cycle
Pocket reference guide used by all to discuss performance; directors coach supervisors on approach to ensure they are holding team accountable	Supervisors and employees better align expectations and more consistently achieve results

Cultural Cross Talk

As organizations increasingly blend and international entities come together, having a common language of leadership and performance can help transcend the many cultural differences that exist and contribute more broadly to strategic alignment.

You may also wonder, "Isn't English the operative lingua franca of business today and isn't that enough?" Certainly most world leaders now speak English in order to communicate with the rest of the world, as do financial wizards, call center operators, scholars, diplomats and just about everybody who is a player in the world economy. Air traffic controllers do too. Ever wonder how a Korean Air pilot communicates to the tower while landing in Paris? Yes, they speak English. The fact is that there are now more English-speaking people in India than in all of North America.

So, while English is literally acknowledged as "the language of business" worldwide, there are still plenty of challenges involved in operationalizing that not-so-simple fact. One of our clients, a long-time pharmaceutical giant with sites in 55 countries, made a formal decision to support 11 core languages. That basically means that all key company communications will be translated into English plus 10 others. The company's managers are expected to be able to speak and understand English. But, the fact remains that translators are still needed for business meetings and training in Tokyo when the participants are from different countries because Japanese is still functionally the language of business there. Yet, every manager in the room could tell you the company's seven leadership behaviors, even if they were shared in seven different languages. Those leadership behaviors have actually been put to the test and passed.

In the best of all worlds, the common language at work would be one in which there is genuine cultural literacy, effective leadership communication and dialogue about performance that is both efficient and adaptive enough to embrace the infinite variety of what can happen out there. I think we still have plenty to learn.

CHAPTER FIVE

GOT TALENT?

It has been astounding to see the shift that has occurred during my professional lifetime in the manufacturing sector of America. Faced with fierce global competition, the US has experienced a precipitous fall from being number one. Plants that once spewed and screeched through three busy shifts a day now stand silent — a graveyard of abandoned equipment and rusty storage tanks. In our journey from an industrial to a service economy, thousands of workers have lost their jobs due to automation and outsourcing of labor. In the past 10 years, about one out of every three manufacturing jobs in the US — about 6 million in total — has disappeared.

Of course in China, the opposite story is happening. Instead of jobs disappearing, potential employees are vanishing. The vast pool of migrant workers from rural areas willing to travel to factories in the large cities is fast drying up. But, their labor shortage numbers in the millions, not just the thousands. In this global economy, where one workforce is flooded, another is drained. Expansion in emerging markets means contraction or stagnation in mature ones. This dynamic is occurring in many industries and professions beyond manufacturing as well.

Wherever you are, and whatever business you are in, you will find that companies are trying to solve this puzzle: how can we both contain labor costs – find and keep the right people – and still make a profit? While the solution remains slippery, we know that talent is a critical variable in that equation. And, when it comes to finding key talent, particularly leaders, there are fierce wars raging. These days, when Facebook's young billionaire CEO Mark Zuckerberg speaks, people listen. On the subject of talent, he recently declared, "Someone who is exceptional in his or her role is not just a little better than someone who is pretty good. They are 100 times better." I don't know if his multiplier is exactly right, but if it is even close, that would mean a serious competitive advantage to the company who lands that exceptional performer.

The Quest for the Best

I'd like to kick off this chapter with a story, a personal one, about looking for talent in a very challenging hiring situation. Back in the 1950s, I became the hiring and training manager for a large aluminum foil manufacturing plant in West Virginia. The plant was set in a tiny town with a population of 300 in a poor, agrarian community. The challenge: I needed to hire 3,000 people! Many of the jobs did not call for skilled labor, and at that time, manufacturing production jobs were relatively easy to fill. However, when it came to looking for a maintenance superintendent, I couldn't find anybody that could really lead the way in keeping all that equipment running. So, I started thinking about who might possibly have the skills that were even remotely related to the job. Then it came to me like "white lightning" – moonshiners! I had heard there were guys up in the nearby hills who had been secretly piecing illicit stills together for years to produce really potent "corn liquor." So, I asked around and went hiking up the hollers past hunting dogs and shotguns looking for them. I probably could have been killed, but at the time, I was just driven to figure it out. And, though it took a lot of convincing, in the end, I got my man. He could fix anything and everything, and proved to be one of the best hires I ever made.

Now, my point in this story is not how great a recruiting manager I was. It is simply that you may turn up talent among people whose profiles do not jump out as exceptional or whose job experience isn't directly related. Today, we are fortunate to have layers of science and research around to help us figure out who might be the best fit.

So, how can you lure and land the best and brightest when everyone else has the same goal? Let's first look at what we know about current workforce planning/talent management practices.

MOST WORKFORCE PLANNING IN US COMPANIES TAKES THE FORM OF:

- A. GROWING TALENT FROM THE INSIDE
- B. ATTRACTING TALENT FROM THE OUTSIDE
- C. SOME OF BOTH OF THE ABOVE
- D. DOING NOTHING UNTIL YOU HAVE TO

Brace yourself. According to recent research, the answer is D – absolutely nothing!

Developing up-and-comers from within is slow and you risk losing them to competitors just when they are "ripe for the picking." Hiring from outside is expensive and has its own set of risks. So, in absence of knowing what to do, it seems that many companies are either ignoring the issue (which dooms them to seeking talent reactively) or waiting to see who figures out what can really work in our world of business uncertainties, so they can then replicate it. Of course, in the meantime, that also traps them in reactivity. And, besides, with this much churn, what succeeds for one industry or company may not necessarily work for yours. Even if it does, it may not work for long.

This quest for the best potential leaders has spawned an entire discipline known as talent management: how an organization attracts, develops and retains skilled people. In our workshops on selecting talent and building bench strength, we emphasize the fact that talent management is not a tactic for reducing turnover or justifying the training budget. Rather, leaders at top-tier companies use it as an essential strategy for achieving the company's most important goals. That strategy could range from something as conventional as internal succession planning to more renegade external "acquiring" – buying a company primarily to capture its exceptional talent. Whatever you choose to do, for the sake of your business survival, let it be more than nothing! Why?

> TWO-THIRDS OF EMPLOYEES AT LARGER COMPANIES EXPECT TO LEAVE THEIR EMPLOYERS WHEN THE RECESSION ENDS. THOSE WITH GREAT LEADERSHIP SKILLS DON'T EVEN NEED TO WAIT.

Growing Talent From the Inside Out

Let's imagine that you are lucky enough to be part of an organization whose leaders demonstrate a committed talent mindset and a strategy that, at least in part, is willing to grow its people from the inside. You then read the same study I just did, which found that while 72% of managers believe that a strong talent pipeline is critical to business success, only 9% were confident that their internal programs would actually deliver one. You may even feel that way without reading a thing. Why?

I believe the problem lies not so much in what organizations are doing but how they are thinking about the issues of developing their people in these times of continual disruption and chaos.

> **TOO MANY INTERNAL DEVELOPMENT PROGRAMS AND TALENT MANAGEMENT PRACTICES RELY ON LESSONS LEARNED FROM THE PAST INSTEAD OF ACKNOWLEDGING THE PREVAILING AMBIGUITY OF TODAY AND TOMORROW.**

We often talk about the **uncertainty** involved in leading a business and developing people today, but **ambiguity** is a more powerful and relevant description. Uncertainty means that you have defined a variable but don't know its value. It is like being dealt a hand of cards when playing poker, but you don't know which cards you have yet. Ambiguity is being dealt a hand of cards but you don't even know which game you're playing or what the figures on the card represent. If your assumptions are based on what skills are needed for jobs in a particular function and who you have in the pipeline, there is a manageable level of uncertainty. But, if you don't know what jobs will exist or what skills they will require, identifying talent that looks promising is far more ambiguous.

A traditional approach to internal development such as succession planning may be built on assumptions that were true in the past but aren't any more. Follow this example with me. Let's assume that you are identified as key talent and are on a succession plan. You begin a development process that will span several years. Yet, during that period, org charts, management teams, the structure of your business unit, even the viability of the business itself changes. Now, an important new vacancy opens up. But, no one on the plan is a fit because that type of job didn't even exist until recently, so you couldn't possibly have been groomed for it. So, now the company looks outside. You and the other internal candidates feel betrayed, and the company's investment in developing you and the others has been wasted. One or more of you may start looking elsewhere now that the implicit promise of opportunity has evaporated. The plan has now gone bust. I'm not catastrophizing when I ask you to imagine this scenario. Just think of where you'd be now if you had recently been on a succession plan at Netflix or Lehman Brothers, K-Mart or Rubbermaid.

So, succession planning, like the five-year business plan, may not be worth it. How do you prepare people for roles that are regularly changing, much less jobs no one knows they need yet? The really agile, alert companies are paying more attention to talent recruitment and retention than ever. They are being creative in the way they are thinking about development and how they identify talent in the first place. I am now seeing talent management models that are based on principles from supply-chain management (talent-on-demand) and agile software development and crowd sourcing. Crazy? No! They are looking past the "HR way" to other business processes that have useful paradigms for rapid change and giving those ideas a try.

> **Case in Point: Modern Day Mad Men**
> In the popular television series "Mad Men," the fictional character, Don Draper, wooed clients to his agency with what was the "new" media of television during the 1960s. Fifty years later, Madison Avenue in New York City is still the nerve center of the advertising world. But, these days, it is Bob Greenberg and his digital ad agency R/GA leading the pack. R/GA's experience flies in the face of the economic downturn. Just last year, the company grew from 1,000 employees to 1,200 and has dozens of openings right now. But, to gain those 200, they actually added 500 new people. No need to check our math. Greenberg and his team engineered a radical reorganization through an incredibly intense transition period. He says he now spends more time than ever on talent retention and recruitment.

How Do You Know a HiPo?

Of course, not every company is bold enough to follow trends on Madison Avenue right away nor should they be. As I said at the beginning of this chapter, what works in one company's talent management strategy may not fit for others.

A much more common practice is investing in the development of high-potential and emerging leaders — and for good reason.

Organizations are investing in their HiPo pipelines as never before. In fact, over 70% of executives in a recent survey indicated they were going to increase their focus on these rising stars. HiPos are often publicly identified in order to reinforce their value, signal the company's commitment to developing them, and hopefully, improve the likelihood of retention – and success – once they transition into leadership roles. They are trained and mentored, offered stretch assignments and executive coaching to prepare and sustain them for the rugged corporate rodeo.

While all this attention is given to the fleeting HiPo, here is a burning question for you:

> WHO IS DEVELOPING THE VAST MAJORITY OF PEOPLE WHO ARE ON HOLD, JUST WAITING FOR SOMEONE TO HAVE TIME FOR THEM?

By definition, HiPos are the few. Everyone else you lead is the many. Unless there is a real commitment to their development, your organization is missing significant opportunities to bring them to their full potential. Accelerating HiPos while ignoring everyone else is an unlikely formula for sustained success. Let's look at a story of one such employee – a seemingly unremarkable guy on the night shift who first went unnoticed by management (not singled out for a HiPo program), then ignored, and finally, gone. But, at what cost?

Recognizing Talent: Reddy or Not?

Once there was a pharmacist who worked the night shift at a large national chain store pharmacy. Reddy Annapareddy thought he had a way to better serve the customers and expand the business: free home delivery and consultation. He was so sure of his idea that he developed a 100-page business plan and drove to

> corporate headquarters without an appointment to try and get it in front of an executive. He managed to get 15 minutes with a VP who quickly dismissed his ideas.
>
> Determined, Reddy quickly quit the chain to pursue his vision on his own. He worked two jobs for two years to save the seed money to start his business, PharmaCare. When Reddy first opened, his store was competing with 25 major chain pharmacies within the same five-mile radius. There was not one item on the shelves in the aisles. When some of the more expensive drugs were ordered, Reddy would fill them by buying them from one of the nearby chain stores that stocked the drug because he could not afford to have them in the inventory. He relied completely on word-of-mouth to get customers and allowed them to pay for their drugs whenever they got the insurance money.
>
> What do you think happened? Well, today PharmaCare is a $50 million-a-year business and one of the fastest growing regional pharmacy networks. Reddy recently won a prestigious national award as Entrepreneur of the Year. And, he brought every member of his staff with him to the ceremony to celebrate.

Would you have taken Reddy's idea seriously? While he was certainly a competent pharmacist, I can assure you there was probably nothing in Reddy's performance review that would suggest he could successfully engineer this prescription for change, singlehandedly implement it and become quickly and solidly profitable.

Let's name some of the qualities that are apparent in Reddy's story and went undiscovered by his former employer:
- Unstoppable drive
- Enterprising spirit
- Unerring focus
- Persistence
- Resilience
- Learning agility
- Compassionate concern
- Antennae for opportunity
- Willingness to adapt
- Business intelligence
- Clear personal values

Now, I am not going to regress to a trait theory of leadership. I'm sure I don't know what experiences and influences led Reddy to have these qualities. But, what I do know is we could see them all in his behavior. And, that's what you need to be able to notice and draw strong conclusions from as a leader. It is part of what we call the "diagnosing" competency in Situational Leadership®. The executive who met with Reddy had behavioral evidence, in just that unexpected meeting, of at least half the qualities on our list above. Just imagine what could have happened if that executive had recognized, encouraged and shepherded Reddy and his idea forward. Unfortunately, that company will never know.

There are things we can learn from those companies who have been committed to developing leaders from within and doing it well for decades. Thriving giants such as IBM and GE have corporate universities that continually equip their top managers and HiPos with evolving leadership skill sets. One of the reasons they continue to have strong business performance is because these programs are not static. At GE, the current head of executive development recognizes that its traditional teams are too slow and that they are not innovating fast enough (again, the diagnosing competency at play). So, she is revolutionizing its leadership training, from redefining what "external" focus means to even changing some of the physical buildings to make them better for teams.

In the next chapter, I'll say more about what to do to develop their capabilities and keep them, so stay tuned or read ahead.

Talent From the Outside In

While it would be great to be able to source everyone you need from within your ranks, it is simply impossible to do. Companies must recruit and hire from the outside too, which poses some even greater challenges in recognizing talent. While the Internet's job search and posting capabilities have opened up countless digital opportunities to communicate what you are looking for, you may be deluged with more inbound resumes but even fewer promising candidates.

What I can tell you for sure is this:

> YOU CAN'T MAKE CHICKEN SALAD OUT OF CHICKEN . . . WELL YOU KNOW, MANURE. PERFORMANCE STARTS WITH SELECTION. PERIOD.

If all people were created equal, great performers or poor performers would not exist. Everyone would do his or her job with equal skill. You may hire the best talent you can find, but if you place them in the wrong job, wrong location or with the wrong boss, that person can quickly become a sub-average performer. Similarly, a less skilled but highly motivated hire may prove to be an exceptional performer if given the right coaching and placed in the right environment.

In Situational Leadership®, when we help managers learn about selecting, engaging and retaining talent, we encourage them to look at three key factors:

- **Readiness**: Can they get the job done? What do people need to do as soon as they begin the job to be minimally successful? This is about their ***baseline skills***.
- **Potential**: What indications are there that they could deliver more or better and positively influence others? Do they have the ***passion, desire and talent*** to go above and beyond? This is the "it" factor: that something extra.
- **Fit**: What do people need to know about the working conditions? Can you describe what it is like to work here? This is about the ***culture***.

The most promising external candidates will be a "yes" to all three of these. The problem is that what you learn most from reviewing applications and interviewing people only addresses the readiness factor. And, potential is often only apparent once you've hired them. You have far more to go on with internal candidates in terms of potential and culture.

Cultural fit is a relatively new part of hiring considerations. There's a saying that goes, "I don't know what fish talk about, but it sure isn't water …" Water is the culture, the environment, that often gets taken for granted but matters an awful lot. A cold-water fish will not thrive in tropical seas! You can't thrive and grow where you don't feel comfortable. That is why so many employers describe the work culture right on their web site, ask interview questions that relate to it, and offer opportunities to talk with people who work there.

Speaking of interview questions, I'd like to call your attention to a best practice known as the "past behavioral interview" (or PBI). You have probably asked or been asked PBI questions such as, "Tell me about a time when you had a conflict with a colleague and how you resolved it." Performance on these kinds of questions always relates to the same three things: experience, job knowledge and social skills. So, they will help you assess readiness, and that is something you have to assess. But, they won't help you get a whiff of potential.

> YOU NEED TO ASK QUESTIONS THAT REQUIRE PEOPLE TO DEMONSTRATE A KEY SKILL BY APPLYING THEIR KNOWLEDGE TO AN AMBIGUOUS SITUATION THAT THE CANDIDATE HAS NEVER CONFRONTED.

What will you learn? Something valuable about the candidate's critical thinking, problem solving, willingness and confidence when faced with something new and unclear. Now, that's highly relevant for facing the business challenges of today and the future. And, their answer will be far more revealing than what they can describe about events in the past.

Here's a simple example that has been used at Microsoft and IBM in interviews for certain technical positions: "Why are manhole covers round?" There's a strong likelihood that they will not know the answer from a skills, experience or knowledge perspective. The answer is: Because they won't fall in the hole and they are easier to move. To answer this question correctly, you need to think about the object's function, risks and benefits of the design, and knowledge of how round things move and be willing to articulate your ideas and what they are based on.

Remember that in ambiguous, complex contexts, we need leaders who can think critically and innovatively to address novel problems. Those thinking skills have been valuable for a long time. That employee who didn't stand out or who doesn't quite fit your mold, might just be the talent you need for a business breakthrough.

CHAPTER SIX

KEEP THEM GOING — AND GROWING

If you are one of the lucky ones — an employee who was not laid off or a manager who didn't have to select those who had to go — since the global economic crisis that began in 2008, you are in the "damn lucky club." The new reality is now settling in: fewer people to do even more work, limited resources and little job security. The emotional climate in many workplaces is now marked more by discontent than fear. A recent Gallup poll reported the major sources of unrest as limited opportunities for growth or advancement (43%), heavy workload (43%), unrealistic expectations (40%) and long hours (39%). So, how can you and your people keep focused forward and giving your best when it is unclear what the future holds for your jobs, careers or the company itself?

It may not be news to you, but not only are we in a global leadership crisis, we are in an employee engagement crisis. Are the two related? You bet! Disengaged employees fall into basically two camps: those who are actively disengaged, voicing their complaints but not going anywhere; and those who are quietly disengaged, tolerating the current state, staying because they are economic prisoners, but looking and beginning to find new opportunities. In either case, their disengagement negatively impacts productivity and organizational performance. And, the really bad news is that the disengaged are staying in their current jobs. The percentage of highly disengaged employees who are actively seeking another job more than doubled in the past half dozen years.

What does that mean for our more engaged and HiPo employees? Layoffs, integrations and the requirement to "do more with less" negatively impacts the productivity, individual motivation and team morale of those who are steadily delivering for you, putting them at greater risk for turnover. Your people are simply not going to perform well unless they are personally engaged. So, you, leader, have a huge challenge to face.

Ignite Their Engagement

First, let's be sure we are clear about what "engagement" really is and isn't. Job satisfaction is a necessary but insufficient part of the equation. It certainly helps if your employees are in jobs that fit their skills, experience and interests. But, fully engaged employees demonstrate commitment and initiative that goes beyond the job description and current performance objectives. This is the land of opportunity! "Discretionary performance" yields results and solutions and ideas that you did not expect. Employees perform not because they have to but because they want to.

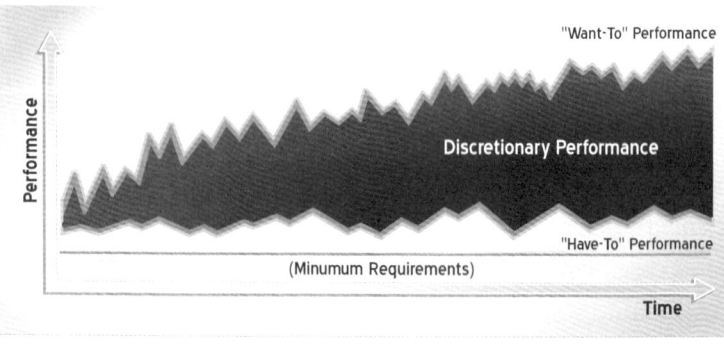

As a leader, you need to build and sustain a critical mass of employees who are doing more than what is required, giving their extra effort when you need it most and focusing that extra effort on your top priorities. Their maximum job contributions, then, are aligned to the company's goals not on an energized, creative, but unrelated, path.

This engagement equation looks deceptively simple. It is, however, easier to describe than to achieve with your people in our current complex contexts.

HOW CAN YOU DRIVE THEIR EXTRA EFFORT? LET'S BE CLEAR: YOU DON'T, THEY DO. YOU PROVIDE THE RIGHT AMOUNT OF DIRECTION, RELATIONSHIP AND THE ENVIRONMENT IN WHICH THEIR ENGAGEMENT CAN FIND TRACTION.

But, our Situational Leadership® core competencies spell out what you can do:

Diagnose: Discover their individual motivations and disengagement triggers around the tasks and goals your team has a responsibility to accomplish.
- What opportunities exist to up your/their game?
- Can you work smarter?
- Can you exceed the goal?
- Can you and your team have greater significance or impact in what you do?
- Where and how can your team have greater added value to other teams?

Adapt: Make changes to your leadership style and the environment.
- Twist the "golden rule" and treat them how they need to be treated.

- Be a match and light some of their fires.
- Make people feel brave.
- Give a little push once in while.
- Let them get their own bumps and bruises (but no broken bones!).

Communicate: Learn to ask them great questions to discover the most important opportunities and problems.
- If you had your choice, what would you do?
- What is standing in your way?
- What will happen if you do and what will happen if you don't?
- What options can you create?

Advance: Provide diverse options and experiences for their development.
- Help them grow their skills to grow their jobs.
- Encourage them to gain horizontal experience and look laterally for career moves.
- Ask them to prove they can handle a promotion by volunteering, helping with interviews, training, coaching and providing feedback to their peers.

DIAGNOSE	ADAPT	COMMUNICATE	ADVANCE
Discover their individual motivations and disengagement triggers.	Make changes to your coaching style and the environment.	Tell them about the most important opportunities and problems.	Provide diverse options and experiences for their development.

For example, imagine that one of your high-performing direct reports expresses an obvious but vague sense of frustration. Through further discussion, he reveals that he thought he'd be less "fenced in" by the need to be at the office on a regular schedule. Diagnosis? He is motivated by autonomy and deserves more of it based on his ability, willingness and results. How can you adapt? Some options might be to: (1) loosen up your level of supervision and stop micromanaging him, (2) offer more flexibility about where and when he or she works and/or (3) provide the technical tools that enable that kind of mobility. Tell him what you plan to do differently and ask him how he could help with any current issues. Ask him what he most needs to learn to make the most of his new degrees of freedom.

Just as I said in Chapter 1 about leadership theories, I have also researched, written and trained thousands of people all over the world about motivation for decades. So, I would prefer to add to my previous thinking rather than repeat it here. Engagement is multifaceted, but motivation is certainly a big gear in the transmission. I've recently come across a number of ideas about how motivation relates to engagement that seem particularly relevant to our leadership challenges today. Therefore, I'll point you to a few of them here and suggest some actions you can take to make a positive difference!

Engagement Focus	If they are wondering ...	You can ...
Path	Where am I headed?	Help them see the way up, around or through
Purpose	What is it all about?	Help them understand the "why?"
Progress	Can I make headway?	Help them set goals and prioritize the "what?"
Problems	What do we need to figure out?	Help them see and solve for them

Path: All Skilled Up and Nowhere to Go

Once there was an almost impenetrable "glass ceiling." It was a very real barrier that blocked the paths of a generation of women and minorities who had strong leadership capabilities from penetrating the ranks of mostly all-male, all-white executives. While progress has been made, the glass ceiling has not been shattered. White males still dominate board memberships and executive roles. Approximately one-half of the boards among Fortune 500 companies were composed of 20% or fewer women and/or minorities.

But, a limited career path is not limited to the top ranks anymore. Some are even asserting that there is no such thing as a career path anymore. Perhaps this is why a 2011 Aon Hewitt global study ranked career opportunities as one of the top three engagement drivers for the past three years. Talented employees who are motivated by achievement or mastery stay engaged when they know their contributions are valued and could lead somewhere. Most managers think "up" when they think about having a career development conversation. Given there is a whole lot more downsizing than hiring going on, many naturally avoid the topic. But, helping employees identify and pursue a career path should really be about exploring many options: lateral moves, special assignments, mentoring relationships or cross-functional projects.

When you realize that your role is still to act as a coach, you can relax and apply what you know about diagnosing readiness for a next career step instead of needing to have a promotion ready. Make a regular point of talking with your employees about how they can also grow through lateral opportunities and broadening their perspective within the same role. You can easily weave engagement discussion points into your one-on-one meetings with direct reports instead of it being a singular event that is part of a formal employee development process. After all, trust is central to developing engagement. Your people need to know that you care about their growth. There is a kind of psychological contract between you and them, so make no promises about a career path or specific future opportunity that you can't keep!

Purpose: Tell Me Why

Our workforce today is populated with as many as five generations of workers. While those in the middle or later stages of their careers are adjusting to the new realities I mentioned at the start of this chapter, for younger workers — the Gen Xers and Millennials — this is their only reality. They don't work to orders or the clock; they work to outcomes and purpose and insist on knowing why they need to do a task or project. And, all employees, regardless of their generation, are seeing that growth depends on what they are able to do, not how long they have been on the job.

In his book "Drive," author Daniel Pink reveals that once the need for reasonable pay is met, people seek three things: autonomy, mastery and purpose. We can see the rise in this motive evidenced by the fact that people with sophisticated technical skills are volunteering significant amounts of their time outside of work and giving away what they develop for free!

But, the importance of finding meaning and discovering purpose is not new and certainly doesn't just belong to only the current younger generation. It becomes particularly keen during periods of great cultural, social and economic distress.

So, it is a good time to refresh our perspectives, as leaders and employees, about what matters most — or what we want to matter most — in our work lives.

We need to be very intentional about helping create a personal and powerful line of sight between the purposes that motivate employees to do the jobs they do. To paraphrase Nietzsche, "He who has a why to work can bear with almost any how." To get the most from their employees, leaders should do all they can to make this "why" clear. The supervisor who can help a baggage handler at the airport see his job as helping a grandmother deliver a gift to her first grandchild or ensuring that she has her medications can inspire a very different commitment to getting her bag through than what he could show from statistics about on-time delivery.

Progress: Pushing the Boulder

Do you ever feel like no matter how much you do, you can't seem to make progress? That experience of unending effort is age-old but perhaps even more keenly felt today. We recognize it in Greek mythology, when the gods condemn Sisyphus to ceaselessly roll a boulder up a steep hill, which tumbles back down each time he reaches the top, for all eternity. When you or your employees suffer from "Sisyphus syndrome" on more days than not, something has got to give before disengagement takes over in the face of futility.

Interestingly, recent research has shown that there is a new motivator in town. It is not recognition or incentives, purpose or career opportunities. Among all the things that can keep people engaged and happy at work, simply making progress on meaningful work has become very important.

Faced with technologies that have many of us navigating between applications and emails on our computers 37 times per hour, making progress indeed seems more and more elusive. The progress motive can also be affected by the relationships between employees and their managers.

> RECOGNITION WITHOUT REAL PROGRESS IS SEEN AS SHALLOW AND PROMPTS CYNICISM. PROGRESS WITHOUT PRAISE IS ALSO DEMOTIVATING.

The combination of making progress, even if it isn't on something big, and getting genuine appreciation from us, as leaders, is a winning combination. And, when there are setbacks, we need to help reframe them as learning opportunities. As John Maxwell has advocated, as leaders and as employees, there are many ways we can "fail forward" without being derailed. You can also help them map out goals and prioritize their activities for progress on meaningful work and say why that progress matters. Can you see the linkage to purpose?

Problems: Being Part of the Solution

The pervasive disengagement in work (and in life) is often met with the popular wisdom to "Follow your passion!" Yet, very little attention is paid to the many stories of those who do follow their passion but never make any money, which just compounds the initial problem. What if we embraced a different antidote and followed our big problems instead? Engagement then becomes less about you or me and more about us and what we face together. We, then, don't have a problem; we become part of the solution and feel more connected to the wider world.

Many of us become more motivated when we can relate to problems on a personal level. A recent workshop attendee told me the story of his neighborhood banding together to stop a landfill from being located nearby. That reality led him to push for even greater recycling efforts at his workplace. "Going green" was then not just a slogan to him. It became a cause and he was part of the solution not only at home but also at work.

This same impulse to engage people in solving problems is part of Google's famous "20 percent time" philosophy which gives its engineers one day a week to work on whatever they want — projects that interest them, tasks that aren't in their job description or a bug that needs fixing. For example, we worked with an R&D director at a major pharmaceutical company whose scientists were struggling to just keep up with their current tasks and complaining of no time to pursue their creative ideas. He empowered a grassroots group of employees to tackle the problem. The outcome? An opportunity for anyone in the unit to request time to develop an idea surrounding new targets, technologies, business development opportunities or pathogens as long as they were rooted in creative science. The selected individuals would ultimately have to present their idea to their manager and group who would decide if it had potential for implementation. You would be amazed at how many people raised their hands and how many ideas were generated!

Growing Into a New Leadership Role

Ongoing development and engagement is one thing. Doing it when you are in transition to a new role is another. It is like trying to bloom when you just got planted! You've no doubt heard of the term "triple threat" when it comes to performing artists. These are the stars that can do it all: act, sing and dance. For new leaders, the triple threat has a very different meaning. They can't yet do it all, so they have to prove themselves in three different ways:

Transition Capability
I will figure out how to get onboard with my boss and my team.

Position Capability
I will learn what it takes to do this job.

Development Capability
I will keep growing my skills as things change and as I change.

NEW LEADERS AT ANY AND EVERY LEVEL NEED TO DEVELOP ALL THREE OF THESE KEY CAPABILITIES IF THEY ARE TO SUCCEED INSTEAD OF STUMBLE.

A deficit of any one of these capabilities, which are unrelated to an individual's existing technical or functional expertise, can derail even the most promising among us. And, if you are a new leader transitioning from being an individual contributor to managing people for the first time, the learning curve is particularly steep (I'll say more about this later). If you have managed others before, position capability may be less of an issue, but the need for transition and development strategies still looms. Let's take a little closer look at each of these.

Making the Transition

Your first hurdle is to actively manage the transition into a leadership role itself. While the job description clearly details what **the** job is, it does not address how to get started in **this** job with this team or this boss at this moment in time. What should my priorities be? How can I get to know my team and their current issues? What are my boss's expectations? How quickly am I expected to deliver changes? Who are my peers and how can I begin building partnerships with them? These are the kinds of key questions that must be clarified before you can really begin to focus on doing the job. And, they point to the fact that effective transition plans are fundamentally about relationship building to include the previous manager, new boss, colleagues and the new team.

Getting the Job Done

Of course you also need to exercise the skills necessary for effectiveness in your new role and do it quickly. However, without a supported transition plan, you can easily sink into leadership quicksand: the business pressure to produce fast results and/or the self-imposed pressure to be fully effective right away. This sense of urgency can lead to "me-driven" mistakes:

It's about me	It's about them
Taking credit	Giving credit
Having all the answers	Asking the right questions
Discounting the perspectives of direct reports	Actively seeking and listening to their views
Withholding information	Sharing information
Myopic instructions	Setting stretch goals

It is natural to want and need to establish our credibility as a new leader. But, if the drive to do so comes from insecurity or ego rather than clarity and confidence, the only thing that is likely to come quickly is trouble.

Getting Out of the Weeds Enough to Keep Growing

As if the transition and position weren't enough to deal with, you also need to continually develop yourself, the team and the organization. Even if you are supremely qualified, your team is high performing and your organization is leading the pack, there is no greater risk than resting on such laurels.

Development capability is really about learning how to learn, being continually ready to recognize what you don't know, to be vulnerable and uncomfortable. That means that stretching your existing skills and building new ones is part of your job — not just a good idea. Like the slogan of the reality TV show, "Survivor," you and your team need to "outwit, outplay and outlast" your competitors as you stare down the ambiguous future.

It is also about building the next level of proficiency within a particular skill set or competency. For example, we know that developing Emotional Intelligence (EQ) is important to becoming an effective leader. That is why the baseline skill of self-awareness and the ability to "read" others is included even at the personal leadership level of our Situational Leadership® curriculum. Next, as a team leader, the strength (or weakness) of your EQ will have increasing relevance and impact on others. It can fuel how effectively you coach your individual direct reports at different levels of ability and willingness. So, we would help you focus on more skilled behavioral observation, performance analysis/evaluation and building group trust and team identity. At more senior levels, EQ will influence your ability to gain buy-in to large-scale changes and encourage organizational learning, even create partnerships with other organizations. This is where we prepare you to assess organizational readiness for the key changes needed and become a competent change leader.

> THE GOAL OF DEVELOPING "LEARNING AGILITY" FOR INDIVIDUALS AND TEAMS AND BECOMING A "LEARNING ORGANIZATION" IS NOW AN IMPERATIVE.

The HiPo Paradox

Maybe you are lucky enough to be a HiPo or to manage one in this relatively job-deprived, talent-starved climate. In either case, while it is flattering to be regarded as an emerging leader, it is also the portal to what we call the " HiPo paradox." Consider this statistic: 70% of high-potential leaders are courted, groomed and subsequently promoted because of their technical prowess and individual results — both of which become immediately, and almost completely, irrelevant in their new roles. Instead, they need to rely on influence, networking, strategic thinking, Emotional Intelligence and resilience as the arsenal of effectiveness. It is as if you were promoted based on your reputation as a solo contemporary dancer and are now expected to choreograph an international dance troupe.

So, what happens? An alarming number — as high as 43.6% according to a Leadership Development Roundtable study — of new-to-role leaders underperform. And, this problem is quickly compounded by the ripple effect that their initial struggles have on others in the organization, dragging productivity in the decidedly wrong direction.

> *"HIPOS" AND NEW MANAGERS, ALIKE, NEED ACTIVE SUPPORT AND GUIDANCE TO ACCELERATE THE SHIFT FROM A "ME" TO "WE" MINDSET AND SKILL SET.*

Let's go back to our example of the contemporary dancer who was selected for a coveted role as a choreographer. She will now have to design the movements of the troupe and not execute them flawlessly as an individual performer. She will have to give directions and not take them. She will have to choose who gets the spotlighted solo and not position herself for the opportunity. What she needs most now are people skills, not technical dance skills, to effectively motivate, facilitate, coordinate, communicate with and influence the members of the troupe. The formula for success has forever changed.

Once you start managing people, the value of your human skills will outweigh and add more value than the technical skills that were once the basis of your proficiency. Research has shown that the greatest impact on leader performance (57.9%) comes from human skills, particularly team building and developing direct reports. Many organizations (perhaps yours) have specific leadership development programs designed to equip leaders at various levels with these vital skill sets. While sending people to training may be a dynamic launchpad for developing people skills, it takes application and follow-up to truly get "lift off" among leaders.

Take that model or tool you learned in class or online and actively use it! We have heard many managers talk about what a difference it made when they pulled out a job aid, such as our pocket reference guide, during a coaching discussion or team meeting to help guide the conversation (see "A Common Language of Performance" in Chapter 4 if you missed it). Don't hesitate to use the tools you've been given.

Being promoted to a more senior level is likely to require more conceptual skills, strategic thinking and business acumen. Consider that our choreographer has now become director of the dance company. Her concerns shift again: How can we sustain our fundraising efforts in the current economic climate? How many new members of the company should we hire this season? How can we capitalize on the current resurgence of interest brought on by competitive dance shows on television? But, as we can see in Katz's model, the ability to think and act with the entire company in mind must be added to the people skills which now become exercised more politically and systemically than in the previous role.

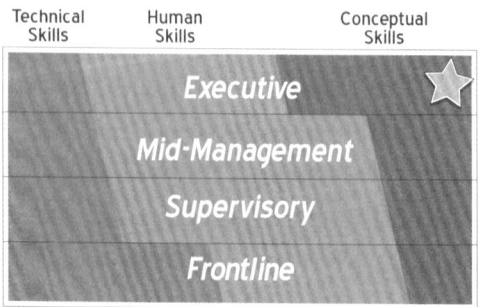

As your leadership journey continues, these cycles will repeat again and again. As your people grow and change, move up and move on, the cycles will repeat. Transition-position-development. Learn-apply-adapt. And never stop growing.

CHAPTER SIX

CHAPTER SEVEN

OUT OF THE DARKNESS AND INTO THE LIGHT

No matter what continent or country you live in, you've heard the story: a charismatic leader falls from grace through scandal. Sometimes the leader resigns or is driven from position or office. Think of the "smartest guys in the room" from Enron. Sometimes he or she hangs on. Think of Italy's Silvio Berlusconi or the leader who recovers and enjoys another round in the spotlight. Think of Bill Clinton. Think of Bernie Madoff. Sadly, prison or suicide may be the result. While the outcomes for the disgraced leaders vary, in every case, those who believed and followed him or her were disappointed and the organization or institution was damaged, perhaps irrevocably.

But, not every leader makes mistakes serious or visible enough to make the news or result in tragedy. More typically, we see missteps and course corrections, gaffs and bad gambles. You may be surprised when I say, "Thank goodness we do!" Because the ability to notice and admit a mistake usually means there is some self-awareness and learning going on instead of image control and cover-ups.

In the previous chapters, I've talked about many of the complex challenges leaders face "out there" from rapid change to plummeting engagement and a scarcity of talent. In this last chapter, I'd like us to look at leaders as very real human beings, warts and all. Too often leaders get elevated, even idolized, by their followers, which makes it hard to admit to being uncertain, wrong or vulnerable. Yet they are. So, let's get real about not only your strengths, which are probably how you got here, but also about your weaknesses, blind spots and emotional triggers.

All Eyes Are on You

It's been said that leaders "cast a shadow" across their organizations through the behaviors we see in them. That shadow can include how they talk, dress, treat others or express their values and beliefs — all of which tend to influence the behavior of their people and the company culture overall.

As I've said for years, "The fish stinks from the head." Of course, in the case of a strong, inspiring leader, the smell would be sweeter!

For example, British magnate Richard Branson's belief in taking big risks is visible in both the success of his Virgin empire and his personal attempts to break world speed records aboard sailboats and hot air balloons. Steve Jobs' devotion to simplicity, incarnate in Apple's product designs, was also seen in the singlular black turtleneck he wore every day. As you can imagine, risk-taking behavior is highly rewarded at Virgin, and you will never see an Apple designer aspiring to an ornate look and feel in the next release.

Now, you may think that attire should have little to do with your credibility as a leader. I did too until the day I showed up for a critical, first meeting with senior leaders at a renowned global company that produces heavy-duty industrial machinery. I walked in wearing a canary yellow "lesiure suit" (as we used to call it) to face a room full of serious suits. I thought I was being so clever wearing something that matched their corporate logo color. The problem was not that I had bad taste (after all, it was the 80s), but that my homework about them was too scanty and missed the mark. I failed to see the shadow and understand their culture until I was in front of the executives. So, why should they have believed that I could understand what they needed and have valuable solutions? I had to work 10 times harder to win them over that day. What is the bottom line?

> **EVERY DAY IN EVERY WAY YOU ARE BUILDING YOUR OWN LEGACY. SO, BE INTENTIONAL ABOUT THE SHADOW YOU CAST, INSTEAD OF JUST LETTING IT HAPPEN.**

Your people are constantly watching, listening and interpreting what you do and say. For better or worse, you are making an impact.

You and Your Shadow

Back in the 1930s, there was a popular radio show that featured a mysterious, unseen crime fighter, known as the Shadow, who had the ability to "cloud men's minds." Each weekly episode opened with the ominous words: "Who knows what evil lurks in the hearts of men? The Shadow knows!" While we know there have been some truly evil leaders; thankfully, they are the exceptions. But, each of us does have other aspects of ourselves that, if unmanaged, can be our unraveling. I am talking about a different kind of shadow than the broad "shadow cast" described above, which could have a positive or negative influence.

In psychological terms first described by Carl Jung, the "shadow" consists of the parts of ourselves that we don't want to see. Why? It may be a part of you that you fear, hate or are disgusted by for some reason. To make matters worse, we tend to "disown" our shadow qualities and behaviors ("That's not me!") and "project" them onto others ("I can't stand that about him!"). Do you find that certain traits in others predictably drive you crazy? Maybe you can't stand it when a coworker doesn't pull their weight or acts egotistically or behaves rudely. Most leaders can recognize these less desirable behaviors in someone else more easily than in themselves. They may be part of your shadow, some aspect of your self-image that doesn't fit, so you push it away (hide it or even denounce it loudly), or reshape it so that it does fit.

Take the case of former New York Attorney General and later Governor Eliot Spitzer. Nicknamed "The Sheriff of Wall Street," he proclaimed, "I want ethics and integrity to be the hallmarks of my administration." Spitzer relentlessly prosecuted crimes by America's largest financial institutions and some of the most powerful executives in the country. Then, shockingly, his shadow was revealed. This paragon of rectitude was caught seeing prostitutes and covering it up.

OUR STRENGTHS STROLL DOWN THE BOULEVARD FOR ALL TO SEE. BUT, OUR SHORTCOMINGS LURK IN THE SHADOW, HOODED LIKE A CELEBRITY WHO DOESN'T WANT TO BE RECOGNIZED.

As a leader, you must be able to accept your shadow, or you will be trapped into feeling and acting like an impostor, continually putting on a façade to conceal that part of yourself. Like the Wizard of Oz, when the grandiose image he has created of himself is exposed as simply human, our first impulse may be to exclaim, "Pay no attention to the man behind the curtain!" But, remember that it was only through exposure that the Wizard was able to impart his gifts to the Scarecrow, the Tin Man and the Lion and free himself and Dorothy to return home.

Remember that your shadow isn't necessarily something you have to root out. We know that Apple's founder Steve Jobs was a perfectionist. He did too. The night before the opening of the first Apple store, he didn't like the look of the tiles so he had them all ripped up and replaced. The engineers of the iPod were pushed to their limits and, as a result, the scroll wheel was inspired. For Jobs, both conviction in his vision — a strength — and his acknowledged perfectionism drove the innovation that led Apple to the top.

Not all of our foibles rise to the level of the shadow. We all keep some things about ourselves private from others, as shown here in the Johari Window Model.

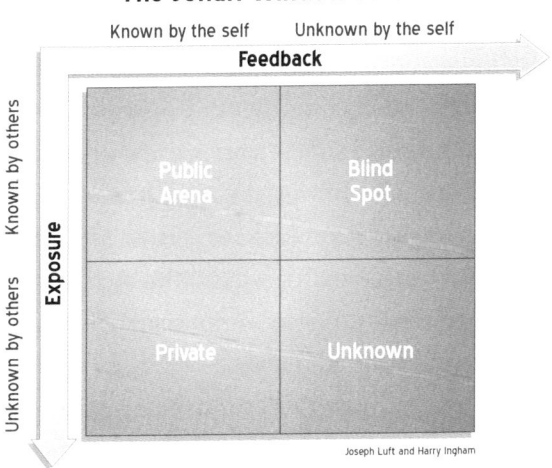

The quadrant called "Private" (sometimes called "Hidden" or "Façade") simply comprises things we know about ourselves that others don't. As a leader, what we disclose and to whom should be a deliberate choice. The people we work with are not entitled to know absolutely everything we think and feel and experience! Yet, disclosure and exposure are ways our self-awareness ("Public Arena") can grow. Building trust and credibility as a leader may involve being more open about yourself, about what you know and about the reasons behind your decisions and actions than you are naturally inclined to be. But, the timing, extent and context of disclosures about you also require critical judgment.

The Blind Side

As both the book and movie "The Blind Side" vividly demonstrate, in (American) football the left tackle's job is to protect the quarterback's blind side from what he can't see coming — defensive linemen! And, so it is with leaders. Our blind side, also called the blind spot, can be seen by others but not by us. Unlike the shadow, which is up to us to disclose, we are utterly dependent on others to provide feedback that allows us to see our blind side (again, see the Johari Window). I believe that those who have the courage to tell us the truth about our behavior function like the left tackle because they protect us – from ourselves. To extend the metaphor: without feedback, ignorance of how we are perceived would keep us fumbling, getting tackled and losing yardage.

Let's look at an example. You are advocating for a particular product choice, but your team doesn't agree with you. Finally one of them says, "You write the checks, so you always win." Recognizing their frustration, you back up and say, 'What I should have said is ..." In that moment, you are moving the Johari Window, enlarging the public arena and slicing away a piece of your blind spot. You know that what you said didn't have the impact you wanted. You can also proactively look for opportunities to shift the size of your window quadrants. You could ask your team, "How could I have said it differently?" That kind of invitation and listening enhances your ability to influence and communicate more effectively.

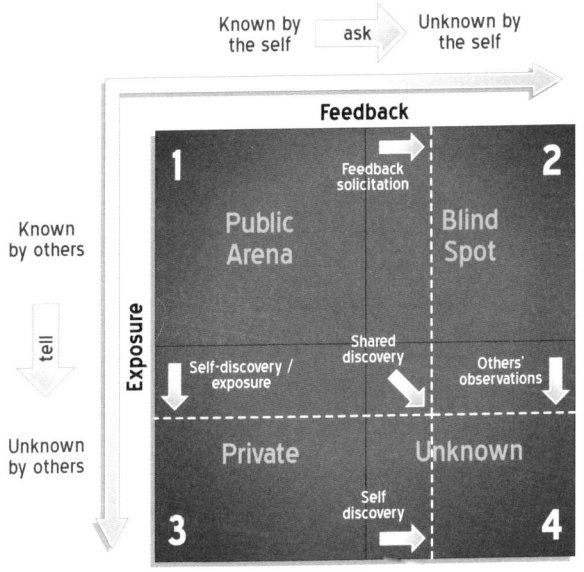

As Peter Drucker once said, "Most leaders don't need to learn what to do. They need to learn what to stop." We need to know about our bad habits and hindering behaviors. The following list of 20 flaws may not be fatal, but they can certainly be damaging to building trusting relationships and getting the most from your people. As you go through it, linger on any that you may have been accused of in the past, even if someone who was upset with you said it.

> **Could any of these behaviors be ones that you need to learn to stop?**
>
> 1. Trying to win the "Who's more miserable?" contest
> 2. Adding too much value
> 3. Passing judgment
> 4. Making destructive comments
> 5. Starting with "No," "But" or "However"
> 6. Telling the world how smart you are
> 7. Speaking when angry
> 8. Negativity or, "Let me explain why that won't work"
> 9. Withholding information
> 10. Failing to give proper recognition
> 11. Claiming credit that we don't deserve
> 12. Making excuses
> 13. Clinging to the past
> 14. Playing favorites
> 15. Refusing to express regret
> 16. Not listening
> 17. Failing to express gratitude
> 18. Punishing the messenger
> 19. Passing the buck
> 20. An excessive need to be "me"
>
> Source: Adapted from Marshall Goldsmith, *Leadership Excellence*

Research tells a consistent story that you need to know; leaders overestimate how positively others see them. You may be fortunate enough to have a manager, peers and/or direct reports who will offer you unsolicited, balanced feedback about both your strengths and your areas for development. If so, count your blessings. Randy Pausch did, even while dying of pancreatic cancer. In his now famous "Last Lecture," this Carnegie Mellon professor shared his childhood dreams and life lessons. One of them came in a moment of getting feedback. His mentor had once said, "Randy, it's such a shame that people perceive you as so arrogant because it's going to limit what you're going to be able to accomplish in life." Pausch fondly noted, "What he was really saying is, 'Randy, you're being a jerk.' But he said it in a way that made me open to his criticisms, to listening to my hero telling me something I needed to hear."

But, I will wager that his experience is the exception rather than the rule. The fact is that you are unlikely to know how others see you unless you ask. Even then, there are many reasons why the feedback you get may be less than candid: perceived power and popularity, lack of trust, fear of retribution, cultural norms and more.

WE ALL TEND TO ACCEPT FEEDBACK THAT IS CONSISTENT WITH THE WAY WE SEE OURSELVES.

WE TEND TO SEE OURSELVES MORE CLOSELY ALIGNED WITH OUR INTENT.

WE ALSO TEND TO REJECT OR DENY FEEDBACK THAT IS INCONSISTENT WITH THE WAY WE SEE OURSELVES.

When you are trying to learn how others see you, instead of soliciting feed*back*, try asking for feed*forward*. My colleagues Marshall Goldsmith and Jon Katzenbach coined the term "feedforward" to encourage a focus on the future rather than on mistakes of the past that cannot be changed. Given the tendency to have an overly positive self-image, leaders tend to resist the negative judgment that comes with feedback but respond favorably to feedforward.

Here's how feedforward works.
- Pick one behavior that you would like to change that could make a significant, positive difference in your life.
- Describe this behavior to someone you trust in a one-on-one dialogue.
- Ask for feedforward: two suggestions for the future that might help them achieve a positive change in their selected behavior. NO feedback about the past is allowed!
- Listen attentively to the suggestions and take notes. Do not comment on the suggestions in any way.
- Thank the other person for their suggestions.

Of course, some of your activities, such as annual performance evaluations, will require feedback that summarizes past accomplishments. But, we have found that leaders in our workshops (on topics such as Emotional Intelligence, self-development, reflection, communication and coaching) enthusiastically embrace the feedforward concept. It provides another way to diminish our blind side by learning and doing differently.

Strengths Overdone

As if having a shadow and discovering your blind side weren't enough to deal with, there is yet another hazard on the leadership highway. We often think of our strengths as our safe haven. Think again. There is a lot of current research that suggests there is more to be gained from spending more time and energy on developing strengths – yours and theirs – instead of trying to overcome weaknesses. But, even your strengths can become a liability. How? Any strength overdone can become a weakness. Huh?

It is possible to have too much of a good thing. In the same way that overusing a muscle group in your fitness workouts can result in imbalances and injury, over relying on certain leadership "muscles" can yield negative perceptions and consequences. Take a look at a few examples below. Have any of your strengths gone "over the edge?"

Strength	Strength Overdone
Sensitivity	Coddling/Enabling/Rescuing
Confidence	Arrogance
Listening attentively	Asking too many questions/Nitpicking
Determination	Ruthlessness
Assertiveness	Aggression/Dominance
High work standards	Perfectionism

Like it or not, as leaders, we too are "works in progress" just like the people we manage and influence. What we need to learn may be a little different but will have a lot more impact because of the nature of our role. So, look in the mirror and be very careful when you answer the question, "Who's the fairest of them all?" The fairest thing you can do is be honest with yourself and ask others to do the same.

Living Out There in the Shadow

We began this chapter by talking about the shadow you cast as a leader. Developing self-awareness is challenging, but let's face it: you are living in the leadership spotlight. Meanwhile, there are many dedicated, stealth performers out there just waiting for someone to notice and really engage them while the HiPos and executives are getting all the attention. So, I encourage you to remember what I have told many leaders: "It is easier to cast a shadow than to live in one."

As you balance your developmental attention between your own and your people's needs, devote some time to helping the solid and steady, if not sensational, workers find their way to the front of the line. They are the quiet majority who have not had the hot projects and just need an opportunity. Making a regular investment of time in each of your people can make such a difference in what they do and how they do it. Like the farmer who arises and goes to the field each morning, we need to take a walk down the halls, check out the climate and see what and who needs our attention most.

Calling All Leaders

As leaders, we are privileged to have a greater span of choices than many — choices that ultimately influence the course of many others and our entire organizations. My hope is that you recognize that being a good leader is a lifelong journey, one in which you will always be both teacher and student, coach and player, artist and scientist. For me, it has been a glorious calling for over 50 years. I am now calling you to step up, to "dig deeper and reach higher" and to map new courses in ways that will make a difference. Your people need you more than ever. Our world needs you to lead and lead better.

About The Authors

Dr. Paul Hersey
Founder and Chairman of the Board
The Center for Leadership Studies

Dr. Paul Hersey's Situational Leadership® has been used to train well over 14,000,000 managers and professional people from more than 1,000 businesses and other organizations. He is an internationally-known behavioral scientist and highly successful entrepreneur.

Professor Hersey is recognized as one of the world's outstanding authorities on training and development in leadership and management. In addition to his teaching, he is a consultant, on a continuing basis, to industrial, government and military organizations.

Dr. Hersey is presently a Distinguished Professor of Leadership Studies at Nova Southeastern University. He is a former faculty member of Northern Illinois University, California State College at Chico, University of Arkansas and Ohio University. Dr. Hersey also served in the roles of Chairman of the Department of Management and Dean of the School of Business, as well as President of California American University – Graduate School of Applied Behavioral Science. Dr. Hersey has also served as Project Director for the Industrial Relations Center of the University of Chicago, Training Director at Kaiser Aluminum & Chemical Company, and manager at Sandia Corporation.

Dr. Hersey has authored or coauthored numerous papers, articles and books including "Management of Organizational Behavior: Utilizing Human Resources," "Organizational Change Through Effective Leadership" and "Selling: A Behavioral Science Approach." His most recent books include "The Situational Leader," "Situational Selling," "Situational Service: Customer Care for the Practitioner" and "Situational Parenting."

In regards to education, Dr. Hersey has received numerous degrees from various institutions including a doctorate from the University of Massachusetts at Amherst, M.B.A. degree from the University of Chicago and a B.S. degree from Seton Hall University.

Diana J. Newton, MA, MED, NBCC

Diana Newton currently acts as a Learning Strategist with Performance Impact where she strategically guides and supports those who seek lasting change for themselves and their organizations. She brings a wealth of experience in leadership development, organizational consulting, executive coaching, facilitation and instructional design to her clients. Her diverse background spans more than two decades in the dynamically evolving pharmaceutical, healthcare and information technology industries. Diana specializes in the area of Emotional Intelligence and integrates related research and applications into the learning events she designs, develops and facilitates.

As a facilitator and leadership coach, she strikes a dynamic balance between group development, personal attention and a well-developed eye for the "big-picture" view of the systems context. Diana's experience creatively bridges the disciplines of business and psychology, bringing great breadth and depth to her roles in classroom and online learning environments and to her writing about the challenges of contemporary leadership.

In addition to consulting and training, Diana spent a number of years as a psychotherapist in private practice. She holds Masters' degrees in English and Counselor Education from UNC-Chapel Hill and NC State University, respectively. She is also credentialed by the National Board for Certified Counselors and is a North Carolina Licensed Professional Counselor.

About The Center for Leadership Studies

The Center for Leadership Studies, founded by Dr. Paul Hersey, is the home of Situational Leadership®. For more than 40 years, CLS has equipped leaders around the globe with the skills to adapt to any circumstance, predict and overcome any challenge, and seize every opportunity.

Situational Leadership® transcends cultural and generational differences and has a success rate that speaks for itself. For example, 70 percent of Fortune 500 companies consider the model a "core, common and critical" component of their leadership development strategy. The Center for Leadership Studies features a diverse line of products and services to include Train-the-Trainer programs, on-site workshops, personal coaching, online training, customized course components, multimedia production and more. You can rely on a single source for all of your leadership development training needs.

At The Center for Leadership Studies – We Build Leaders™!

Connect With CLS

Facebook
Like us on **facebook.com/WeBuildLeaders**, where you can chat with a diverse group of professionals, including thought leaders, trainers, executives and frontline practitioners from a variety of different industries. Hear first-hand about the benefits of utilizing Situational Leadership® from CLS clients and access a variety of multimedia content.

Twitter
Follow us **@WeBuildLeaders** for the latest research, news and tips on using Situational Leadership® to transform your organization.

YouTube
Watch the Situational Leadership® experts in action at **youtube.com/WeBuildLeaders** and learn more about the most widely used leadership model in the world.

LinkedIn
Join the conversation and network with the brightest minds in the industry at the Situational Leadership® group on LinkedIn.

Blog
WeBuildLeaders is your ultimate resource for Situational Leadership® articles, videos and foundational material. Access information you won't find anywhere else at **situational.com**.